FENG

SHUI

QUICK GUIDE

for Home and Office

Secrets for Attracting Wealth, Harmony, and Love

FENG

SHUI

QUICK GUIDE
for Home and Office

CAROL M. OLMSTEAD, FSII

Carol M. Olmstead

Feng Shui Multimedia
Santa Fe, New Mexico

Feng Shui Quick Guide for Home and Office:
Secrets for Attracting Wealth, Harmony, and Love
By Carol M. Olmstead, FSII
Published by: Feng Shui Multimedia
369 Montezuma Avenue, Suite 526
Santa Fe, NM 87501

Cover and interior design by Pneuma Books, LLC. Visit www.pneumabooks.com
Additional illustrations by Jaye Oliver Designs

Publisher's Cataloging-in-Publication Data

Olmstead, Carol M.
Feng Shui quick guide for home and office: secrets for attracting wealth, harmony, and love / Carol M. Olmstead. -- 1st ed. -- Santa Fe,
NM: Feng Shui Multimedia, c2008.

p. ; cm.

ISBN: 978-0-9815735-0-2
Includes bibliographical references.

1. Feng Shui. 2. Room layout (Dwellings) 3. Office layout. I. Title.

BF1779.F4 O46   2008 2008923043
133.3/337--dc22   0809

14 13 12 11 10 09 08   10 9 8 7 6 5 4 3 2 1

For my husband, Tom,
with love for always being there;
for Ben and Jill for encouraging me to write this;
for Sammy and Isabelle,
for being my most pleasant distractions from writing.
And for my mother and father.

ACKNOWLEDGMENTS

This book could not have been written without my clients, students, and e-zine readers, who provided the inspiration. With gratitude to my clients, for sharing their stories and opening their homes, offices, and businesses to me; my students, from whom I learn with every workshop I teach; and my readers, whose questions keep me on my toes.

Special thanks to my two Mastermind groups for reading sections and offering their wise comments and complete support throughout the process of writing this book. In Maryland, thanks to Wendy Epstein, Beth Smith, and Sharon Dooley. In Santa Fe, I'm grateful for the support of Beverly Croydon, Janet DiLuzio, and Susan Wazzan. I will rely on all of you for help with the next book. Thanks, of course, to Anne Sanderoff-Walker for always being my rock.

I am doubly blessed to be doing the work I love and making so many friends along the way.

CONTENTS

The three rules of work:
1. Out of clutter, find simplicity.
2. From discord, find harmony.
3. In the middle of difficulty lies opportunity.
~ Albert Einstein

FOREWORD

With the exception of a few survivalists and nomadic herders, most of us spend the vast majority of our lives in environments that are influenced by human activity or designed and built by humans. Cities and towns, houses, office buildings, and factories are all part of the daily experience of our lives. So too are the individual rooms in our homes and places of business. Each of these places has a distinct set of characteristics, and each of these places can exert a profound influence on the quality of our lives. More important, each of us knows and feels the influence of our built environment. Although we cannot always articulate why, certain places make us uncomfortable, while others are simply "just right."

Of course, understanding the "why" of our built environment is important, since we all want to re-create the places and environments that make us feel most at ease and contribute to our growth, as individuals and as entire communities. This need exists at all scales, from individual rooms to entire metropolitan areas.

For example, we know that the layout and design of our cities can strongly influence public health, fiscal and economic vitality, and the quality of the natural environment within and around those cities. In some cases, a town or county can start from a clean slate and can comprehensively envision and plan its future with these goals in mind. In other cases, improved quality of life involves a delicate negotiation of the fixed and fungible elements of the city's layout and infrastructure. For urban planners, successfully executing this balancing act can translate the community's loftiest goals into reality.

Feng Shui seeks to achieve many of the same goals within the smaller-scale environment of individual homes, offices, and rooms. Indeed, the successful application of Feng Shui is much akin to urban planning. It involves balance in the visual and physical characteristics of the room and the home in question.

The tools, of course, are different. For the planner and designer, it may be zoning codes or building design guidelines, streetscape plans, or the design of a park or recreational trail. For the Feng Shui practitioner, it may be furniture, paint, plants, or artwork. (In both cases, a little bit of cleanup can also go a long way!) Nonetheless, in many cases, the fundamental concepts at work in planning and Feng Shui are remarkably similar.

For example, in Feng Shui the square is the symbol of stability, balance, and well-being, while the rectangle is the symbol of growth

PREFACE

This book began as a fifteen-page, spiral-bound workbook I created in the mid-1990s for clients of my Feng Shui For Real Life consulting practice. As I began to work with more and more people, it quickly became obvious that while all of them were intrigued, many were also somewhat confused or intimidated by Feng Shui. Much of this confusion resulted from the explosion of books on Feng Shui, each relating to different approaches and schools of thought.

My clients obviously needed one source of clear, concise, and easy-to-follow advice on how to make this ancient practice relevant to their contemporary world. That original workbook was also born out of my desire to explain why I recommended certain changes in their homes and offices rather than expecting my clients to blindly follow my advice.

Now, with the urging of my many clients and students, I have expanded my original workbook into this *Feng Shui Quick Guide for Home and Office: Secrets for Attracting Wealth, Harmony, and Love* to share the practical magic of Feng Shui with more people than I can possibly reach through my practice. And to thank my clients for their encouragement, I have sprinkled their success stories throughout the pages to illustrate how everyday people made everyday changes to truly improve their lives.

After more than a decade of studying and teaching Feng Shui, people call me the Feng Shui Maven because I have developed a means to easily bring the essence of this practice to others in a way that is not only powerful, but fun. My method of Feng Shui consulting, called Feng Shui For Real Life, bridges the gap between centuries of Feng Shui knowledge and the real-life challenges of living in today's world. Now, in this *Feng Shui Quick Guide*, I present the basic tools most people need to place furniture and objects in the right position to bring wealth, harmony, and love into their lives. In addition, this book shows how a few strategic Feng Shui improvements can remove blockages and open up new worlds of possibility. At the end of the book is a calendar of daily tips for using Feng Shui in your home and office throughout the seasons of the year.

A few recommendations for using this book.

First, don't let words like *Feng Shui*, *chi*, or *bagua* confuse you. You already intuitively feel the principles that I talk about, even if the terminology is initially confusing. This book will give you explanations for those feelings — good and bad — that you have about your indoor surroundings. Additionally, you will come to understand why sometimes you walk into a restaurant, store, office, or rooms of your own home and feel good, but resist walking into others because they feel so bad.

Second, sometimes we arrange our furniture and objects in a way that blocks good things from coming into our lives, and sometimes we are emotionally blocked and arrange our surroundings to mirror that blockage. Either way, we don't get what we want in life.

No matter which situation you find yourself in, a few strategic Feng Shui improvements will remove the blockage and open up your world to amazing possibilities. I have seen hundreds of clients make simple changes in their homes with startling, positive results.

I recommend you work through this book in the order that the chapters are presented so that by the time you get to the calendar of tips in the last chapter you will have the background knowledge to understand why I recommend them. It's okay to peek and experiment with a few tips from the calendar, but I urge you to return to the chapters in the book before you undertake a complete year of Feng Shui improvements. You will reap the full benefits if you first understand the basics of Feng Shui.

This black-and-white book by definition uses black-and-white graphics; however, we live, work, and play in a world that is full-color. To reconcile the two, I direct you to my website, *www.FengShuiForRealLife.com*, where you can see and download color versions of many of the graphics in this book from the *Basics* section on the site.

When I show up at their front door, clients frequently tell me they have been confused and intimidated by the Feng Shui books they have read. But after the consultation almost everyone tells me they had fun. Through this book I invite you to experience the same fun, power, and practical magic of Feng Shui. From start to finish, I hope you will experience Feng Shui as an amazing way to bring positive energy flow into your home and office, and as an easy and enjoyable way to improve your life.

Enjoy!

Carol M. Olmstead
Santa Fe, New Mexico

PART ONE

Feng Shui For Real Life — More Than Smoke and Mirrors

There's no place like home.
~ Dorothy

FENG SHUI
TO THE RESCUE

*I think that when you invite people to your home,
you invite them to yourself.*
~ Oprah Winfrey

Susan was in a panic when she came into my Feng Shui class. A successful real estate agent specializing in high-end properties, she was having some unexpected trouble selling a particular house. She turned to me, the Feng Shui Maven, for help.

"I just don't understand why it doesn't sell," Susan admitted after class. "It's a great property. Luxury brick townhouse. Upscale community in a prime location. The owner is a clean freak, so it shows like a model: granite counters, hardwood floors, upgraded carpet. But I'm not even getting low-ball offers. What can help me sell this house?"

A luxury house that isn't selling in what was then a red-hot real estate market? A market so sizzling that even *fixer-uppers* were selling in a day for shocking prices? I knew that there was only one answer to Susan's question: *Feng Shui*.

"Tell you what," I offered, "I'll take a look at the house and give you some free Feng Shui advice. My husband and I are starting to think about moving from our five-bedroom house to a smaller one, maybe a townhouse, so this will be an opportunity for me to see just how much downsizing we might have to do in the future."

Susan perked up and asked, "You are selling your home? Where is it located and how much are you asking?"

I gave her the location and, off the top of my head, named a high, but fair, figure.

Susan barely hesitated when she replied, "I have a buyer coming in from California who's been looking in your neighborhood and price range for the past three months. He's starting a new job and needs to get settled quickly. Can I bring him by on Monday night for a one-time showing of your house? If he buys the house, I'll cut my commission in half."

What could I lose? We shook hands.

Fast forward to Monday. In anticipation of showing our house I moved twenty-seven things, a standard Feng Shui *cure* for revving up prosperity energy in a home (see "Calendar of Feng Shui Tips," January 1).

The doorbell rings. It's Susan with the prospective buyer. Let the house tour begin!

Fast forward again, this time to Wednesday evening. I signed a contract to sell our house at an amazing profit. I was thrilled and the buyer was relieved.

The next day, as promised, I took a look at the house Susan had been trying to sell. It was the only townhouse in the community without a deck, which made it look smaller and insignificant in comparison to the others. I recommended to Susan that the owner quickly get a contractor's estimate to build a deck, include that written estimate with the house promo materials, and offer to reduce the asking price by the cost of the deck.

Within two days of the estimate's arrival, the house sold. Susan was delirious.

Feng Shui (pronounced *fung shway*) is the art and science of placement. Sometimes good Feng Shui is just common sense, while other times it works in almost unimaginably mysterious ways. And when you make Feng Shui changes, you always get what you *need* — even if it isn't what you think you *want*.

Feng Shui first came into my life in the late 1990s when I was a public relations consultant running a successful home-based business. Now, after coaching and teaching thousands of people, writing numerous articles, giving countless speeches, and participating in television, radio, Internet, and print interviews, I'm the Feng Shui Maven who has introduced Feng Shui to my clients and students. And now I'm introducing it to you.

My friend Jean brought me my first book on Feng Shui, which she picked up from the sale rack at Barnes and Noble.

"This *feng shoe-y* is confusing," Jean admitted (we didn't know how to pronounce it then, either). I poured over the complex advice in the book, befuddled by diagrams of baguas, descriptions of flying stars and trigrams, and compass points where south is up and north is down. The more I read, the more confused I became.

"I'm not sure," Jean cautioned, "but it looks like your desk is facing the wrong direction." In Feng Shui, the most *inauspicious* position for a desk is sitting with your back to the door. In this position, your competitors, clients, and colleagues can actually and symbolically catch you off guard. The symbolism is obvious: things go on behind your back.

And there I was, sitting with my back to the door, facing the two windows. So, to humor my friend, we turned around my desk so I was facing the door on a diagonal. I could still see out one window so it wasn't such a bad view. I agreed to give it a try. Off we went to lunch, and I didn't think much more about Feng Shui.

Two weeks later I signed a contract to consult in Honolulu for a week.

And the next thing I knew my laptop and I were on the soft sands of Waikiki as I worked out the finer points of the campaign I would propose to my client. I presented the campaign and the client was pleased. Just how pleased, I was about to find out.

"There's one more person who needs to hear your advice," he explained, "but he won't be back until next Thursday. Can you stay?"

Can I stay?

In paradise for a second week?

In February?

I told him how much it would cost for me to stay another week. "See you next Thursday," he replied.

The presentation was a success and the campaign was approved.

Back home in the icy Northeast I reflected on my good luck in getting the consulting job in Hawaii. *What made it happen?* I didn't market to this client differently than I would to other clients. I didn't change my presentation techniques. Could it have been the fact that I made one simple change in the placement of my office furniture? Was it simply luck, or had my Feng Shui improvement been responsible for my good fortune? Was there more to Feng Shui than *smoke and mirrors?*

So I started reading about Feng Shui, and the more I read, the less I understood and the more confused I became. I enrolled in a Feng Shui course and that was all it took — I was hooked. I continued my studies, earned a Feng Shui practitioner certification from the Feng Shui Institute of America in 1998, and have been practicing ever since.

Based on my experience with Feng Shui, I have culled for this book the basic tools and tips that most people need to make Feng Shui work for them. I'll show you how to place your stuff — the stuff you already own and love, and the stuff you want to acquire — in the right position to bring wealth, harmony, and love into your life.

Occasionally I hear concerns from people who contact me after having tried some Feng Shui techniques from complicated books they don't understand or advice from online Feng Shui gurus who reviewed their floor plan via e-mail. They say things like:

I moved my bed, bought a plant, added a fountain, cleaned out my closet, but nothing is happening. Okay, that's not quite true. Good things are coming into my life, but I haven't been invited into the private banking department of my bank yet, I don't have the corner office, and I haven't found the love of my life. Why isn't Feng Shui working?

The awareness that Feng Shui gives us about how our interior surroundings affect our well-being and success can greatly improve our lives. But Feng Shui won't fix all of our problems or save us from all the pitfalls of life. Feng Shui can come to our rescue, but we have to meet it halfway to benefit from all it has to offer. Almost 90 percent of the results from adjustments you make in your home or office come from the power of your intention to make a change. If you are blindly making Feng Shui changes because you think you *should*, you will not get the anticipated results because you lack strong intention. As the saying goes, it will be just another case of *shoulding* on yourself.

It's like a really bad light bulb joke: *How many Feng Shui practitioners does it take to help you change a light bulb? Only one, but the light bulb really has to want to change.*

Although this book provides much Feng Shui advice and many tips for improving your life, for Feng Shui adjustments to work for you, you need to be ready to make a change in your life. Among the thousands of clients and students I have worked with, I often find that people put up the most resistance to the changes they most need to make. Have they arranged their furniture and objects in a way that blocks positive improvements from occurring, or are they emotionally blocked and have arranged their furniture in a way that mirrors that blockage? Like the chicken-and-egg dilemma it truly doesn't matter which came first, it only matters that you have the *intention* to change your life and take action to make the appropriate adjustments in your interior surroundings — and make a difference in your life.

Here are some of the reasons why people resist making the everyday Feng Shui adjustments that, deep down, they know will make a difference:

- **People have a natural resistance to change.**
  People like things to stay essentially the way they are, even though this is at odds with the natural rhythm of life, which is constantly in a state of change. Change is natural, and making Feng Shui adjustments can help you accept change as part of the cycle of life.

- **People see only what they want to see.**
  We have selective vision and tend to ignore what doesn't please us. Our dreams and desires sometimes blind us to what we already have accomplished. For example, even if business improves in a slow but steady pace, we complain because we didn't land the multi-million dollar contract yet. We tend to see failure where there is actually success.

- **People may not be ready to accept change.**
  Sometimes we want something but we actually aren't ready to accept it, or in the long run it wouldn't benefit us. If you are supposed to do something, the universe will clear the way for it to happen; but if you're not supposed to do

something, the universe will place obstacles in your path to encourage you to find another route to achieve your goal. Everything happens in its own time.

Feng Shui works best when you focus on improving a specific aspect of your life — such as finding a new romantic partner, increasing your cash flow, or locating the perfect new job. Targeting a specific goal allows you to focus on the areas of your home or office where Feng Shui improvements will be most effective. It's also helpful to remain flexible about the results of Feng Shui changes since there might be an even better possibility that you haven't imagined.

In general, when making Feng Shui improvements, I recommend that you focus clearly on what you want to change, then trust that the universe will bring you exactly what you need, even if that turns out to be something different from what you anticipated.

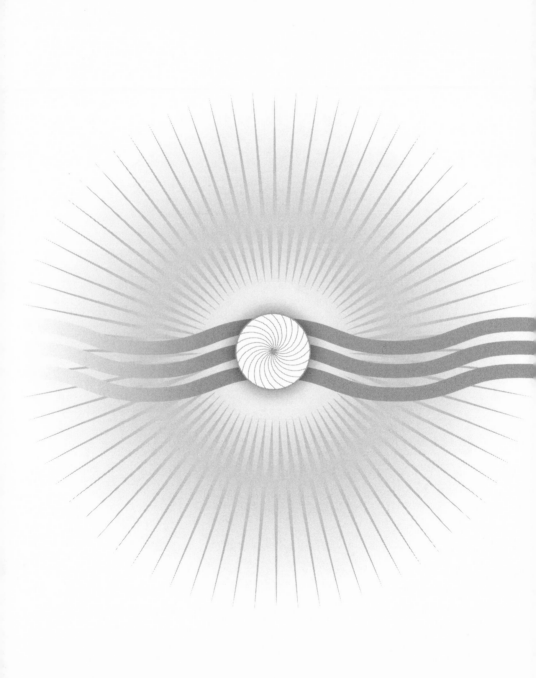

CHAPTER 2

A PRACTICAL
MAGIC APPROACH

The thing always happens that you really believe in;
and the belief in a thing makes it happen.
~ Frank Lloyd Wright

The practical magic of Feng Shui is different for each of us, but when people find out I am a Feng Shui practitioner, they typically ask the same four questions.

How Do You Pronounce Feng Shui?

Feng shu-y, veng shu-y, fung-shoe? The first question is the simplest to answer: you pronounce it *fung shway*.

What Is Feng Shui?

Feng Shui is the art of placing things around you in balance and harmony with the natural world. Our indoor environment has a powerful effect on what we attract into our lives. When the energy, or chi (pronounced *chee*), around us is blocked or unbalanced, our prosperity, health, and relationships can be adversely affected. Feng Shui is like acupuncture for your home, unblocking the flow of positive energy, removing negative energy, and allowing you to achieve your goals – without using any needles.

Want to earn more money or grow your business? Yearning to rev up your love life? Looking to encourage family harmony in your household? Need to control clutter before it controls you? Or do you just need a good night's sleep? Feng Shui improvements in your home and office can bring all of this and more.

Based on a 5,000-year-old Chinese art and science, Feng Shui evolved as people saw how their surroundings determined whether they would just survive or thrive. In ancient China, people planned cities in concentric rectangles surrounded by walls that were flanked by lakes, hills, valleys, gardens, courtyards, and parks. As people moved from agrarian to urban societies they modified this Feng Shui planning to fit their environment, resulting in several major schools, or approaches, to Feng Shui. This gives the modern practitioner in our Western culture a range of techniques and tools to use during a home, office, business, garden, or real estate consultation. But it can leave the casual dabbler confused by all of the seemingly contradictory information.

Feng Shui isn't a religion or superstition. Rather, it is the art and science of keeping your indoor environment balanced. Feng Shui isn't a magic pill, but rather it's a serious and profound system and technique. The contemporary, practical approach to Feng Shui in this book is based on common sense, good design principles, regional geography, and a lot of my experience and intuition. Feng Shui works in any built environment. It's a simple matter of placing the right objects, colors, and shapes in the right locations to achieve harmony with nature and with yourself.

My clients tell me they have fun making their Feng Shui adjustments and clearing their clutter, then watching — sometimes with surprise — as wonderful things start to flow into the space they have created for it. When Feng Shui changes are made in the right way for how *you* want to live your life in *your* home and work in *your* office…everything just feels better.

Now it is your turn. And with this book, the process is going to be easy.

The changes are sometimes obvious, sometimes subtle, but you will immediately feel the difference in your surroundings. That's why I call it *practical magic*. A few simple, low-cost, and real-world Feng Shui adjustments for your home, workplace, or business can help you attract wealth, harmony, and love in a way that seems almost magical.

Will Feng Shui Fit My Culture?

Even though the roots of this ancient practice are Chinese, Feng Shui improvements can be made to fit all cultures and all decorating styles. You don't need to decorate your home in an Asian decor to appreciate order and harmony, because Feng Shui-like advice runs through various cultures. Serenity knows no single culture. We experience Feng Shui cultural crossover all around us without even realizing it.

When my cousin Arlene gave me a set of steak knives as a wedding shower gift, simultaneously, my Jewish mother, grandmother, and aunt reached into their purses and pulled out pennies.

"You have to give Arlene a penny to keep the knives from cutting your friendship," Grandma ordered.

I complied, not really understanding, but vowing never to give anyone a set of steak knives as a gift. I now know that although she didn't realize it, my grandma was practicing Feng Shui, because a classic Feng Shui recommendation is to avoid giving gifts with sharp edges, like scissors, knives, or swords, because these objects symbolize the cutting of a relationship (see the "Calendar of Feng Shui Tips," December 9).

A few years ago, I was privileged to observe a Native American ceremony at a ground-breaking to begin construction of a new building. The Shaman began by lighting a sage bundle and using eagle feathers to push the smoke around the site. He explained that sage removes bad spirits and brings good spirits and energy, then asked permission from the earth to build on the site. The Shaman explained that without proper granting by the earth and honoring the earth it may not be a good building. Workers might get hurt during construction, people won't like working in the building, and it could be a sick building.

Similarly, in Feng Shui we clear a home of any negative energy by using smoldering sage, which we push into the four compass directions using a feather. We use positive affirmations to ensure that only good energy will surround the occupants.

When I lived in the Washington, D.C., area in the 1980s, one of my favorite restaurants in upper Northwest was called Mr. T and Son. When you sat down they handed you two menus: one Chinese food and the other classic Jewish deli selections. I could order my dream meal — a bowl of chicken soup with a side of egg rolls, complemented by a pickle from the bowl already on the table. You didn't have to be Chinese or Jewish to love that meal, and that's how I think of contemporary Feng Shui: a blending of the best of many cultures.

Why Do You Call It Feng Shui For Real Life?

As Feng Shui evolved and spread to different countries, various cultures put their own interpretation on its practice. That's why there are now as many approaches to Feng Shui as there are to architecture or interior design.

If you are new to Feng Shui, this could mean a lot of confusion when you try to do it yourself. The major schools of Feng Shui use some of the same basic principles, but each has a different approach. For example, Form School focuses on the auspicious positioning of buildings in regard to the landforms around them. Compass School uses a compass to decide auspicious and inauspicious locations for buildings, floor plans, and room layouts. Black Hat School (also called Black Sect) focuses on the positioning of shapes and the use of color.

If you read too many Feng Shui books or articles with advice from too many different schools, you will come away with seemingly contradictory advice (and maybe eye strain). While the "cures" and adjustments from the various schools of Feng Shui have validity when used by practitioners trained in those particular disciplines, you don't need to know them all to use Feng Shui to design your own personal balance and harmony and to fix anything that is wrong with your real life.

Lately, there is a lot about Feng Shui in the print and broadcast media. Developer Donald Trump, Las Vegas mogul Steve Wynn, Virgin Airlines founder Richard Branson, and fashion designers Donna Karan and Tommy Hilfiger use Feng Shui. Chase Manhattan Bank, Citibank, Coca Cola, Dow Jones, Hyatt Hotels, Lucent Technologies, Mercedes Benz, Canon Europe, Microsoft, Motorola, Shell Oil, The Body Shop, Universal Studios, and the Wall Street Journal have used it to rapidly expand their business. Their employees are happier and, consequently, more productive, which improves the bottom line.

The British tabloids have rumored that Prince Charles and other members of the royal family, as well as former Prime Minister Tony Blair, have all sought help from Feng Shui experts.

Celebrities have long been associated with using Feng Shui to transform their careers. In fact, Hollywood has been called ground zero for Feng Shui, with supporters including Oprah, Madonna, Johnny Depp, Pierce Brosnan, Sting, and Demi Moore.

In the movie *Bridget Jones' Diary*, Bridget *feng shui-ed* her trash can and found her Mr. Right. In an episode of the TV show *Sex and the City*, Carrie Bradshaw explains friend Charlotte's Feng Shui approach to dating as "change location, change luck."

All of these media images of Feng Shui *magic* are sometimes hard to believe. It feels like a lot of mystical smoke and mirrors. And most of us don't inhabit the rarified worlds of celebrities like "The Donald." We are just trying to make the best out of our real lives.

What has been missing in all of this hoopla about Feng Shui is advice focused on how *you* want to live in your home and work in *your* workspace. That's why I call the Feng Shui approach in this book *for real life*. When I provide recommendation for clients, I consider each person's goals. I suggest practical, appropriate, and workable solutions that are based on solid Feng Shui principles, fit with the way you live and work, and match your style and budget. My approach is the same in this book, where I present tips and techniques that you can customize for the real life you live.

For so many people, Feng Shui is intriguing but intimidating. What has been missing is a user-friendly, easy to understand explanation of this art and science that makes it simple for you to make daily, basic changes to achieve the results you want.

It all starts with understanding the basics of Feng Shui.

PART TWO

Understanding the Basics

We shape our buildings: thereafter they shape us.
~ Winston Churchill

CHAPTER 3

THE HEART OF FENG SHUI

The wind is mild, the sun is warm,
The water is clear, the trees are lush.
Such a spot has good Feng Shui.
~ Ancient Chinese Proverb

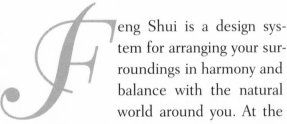

Feng Shui is a design system for arranging your surroundings in harmony and balance with the natural world around you. At the heart of the practice of Feng Shui is the desire to bring people in balance with their indoor, or *built*, environments to attract good health, prosperity, and better relationships.

The Chinese words *feng* and *shui* mean *wind* and *water*. To understand this better, picture a beautiful May day. The sun is brilliant in a cloudless blue sky. There is a light breeze tickling your skin as you relax by a meandering clear stream. In that kind of environment, you feel wonderful. Your creativity is in high gear, you can solve any problems, figure out any issues troubling you. If you are with your spouse or partner, well, let's just say that nature will take its course and it's pretty romantic. If you are with your children or family, everyone is happy and having a wonderful day.

Why shouldn't your indoor environment make you feel the same way? That's the goal of Feng Shui changes for your home or office — to connect your indoor space to the natural world around you in a way that makes everything feel harmonious. Feng Shui unblocks and corrects any imbalance around you to let positive energy flow into your life. Once that happens, you are more receptive and responsive to the good things that come your way.

Major Schools of Feng Shui

The major schools of Feng Shui use some of the same basic principles, but each has a slightly different approach. Some practitioners use a compass, others incorporate astrology and numerology, and most use a *bagua* (pronounced *bag-wha*), which is simply a mapping chart used in Feng Shui analysis of a space.

Here are a few of the more common methods of using Feng Shui:

- **Feng Shui For Real Life** is a contemporary, real-world, and intuitive approach that focuses on how you want to live in your home and work in your office. This book is based on the Feng Shui For Real Life approach and orients the bagua map from your front door.

- **Form School** focuses on the auspicious positioning of buildings in regard to the landforms around them.

- **Black Hat (or Black Sect) School** is a hybrid of Tibetan Buddhism, Taoism, and Chinese Feng Shui that focuses on placement of shapes and use of color.

- **Compass School** uses a special compass called a *lo-pan* to determine auspicious and inauspicious locations for buildings, floor plans, and room layouts.

- **Flying Star Feng Shui** is based on star movements, and corrections are placed to destroy, protect, or use up ill-placed stars.

- **Pyramid School Feng Shui** is a Western adaptation of ancient Chinese Feng Shui, integrating biology, psychology, cultural anthropology, physics, and environmental factors.

- **Yin House Feng Shui** is used in Asia for grave sighting, where it is believed that the placement of an ancestor's grave will have a direct impact on the fortune or misfortune of the family for generations.

Closely related to Feng Shui is *vastu*, the philosophy from India that involves designing a home or building to align it with the sun to take advantage of natural light throughout the day.

When Do I Use Feng Shui?

I recommend you make Feng Shui adjustments whenever you feel dissatisfied with your personal life or professional career or if you are not getting what you want out of your life. Feng Shui adjustments for your home can help you increase wealth; attract love; improve health; reduce stress; unblock creativity; conquer clutter; find a better job; increase business; and buy, sell, or remodel a home or building. Can you find something you want in that list?

Some situations that can benefit from Feng Shui adjustments include:

- Moving into an existing home, office, or business location.

- Designing or building a new home.

- Remodeling, redecorating, adding an addition, or undertaking major landscaping.

- Selling a home, a building, or land.

- Moving in with a partner or roommate.

- Going through a major life change, such as marriage, the birth of a baby, divorce, illness, retirement, or financial gain or reversal.

On the job, whether you work in a corner suite, a cubicle, or a home-based office, Feng Shui can improve your career success and increase job satisfaction. Feng Shui considerations become especially important for home-based businesses, where your home and workplace are tightly linked, since experiences at work cannot be isolated from your experiences at home. Many Feng Shui adjustments for an office are inexpensive, involving simple actions such as rearranging furniture, using color and texture, adding personal items, correcting the lighting, and reducing clutter.

The Five Power Principles

There are five powerful principles you need to understand before you can start using Feng Shui to attract wealth, harmony, and love into your life. I will explain each of these principles in detail in the next few chapters:

1. **Chi** (the energy around you).

2. The **Five Elements** (the colors, shapes, and textures you choose).

3. The **Bagua** (a mapping chart you use to decide where to place colors, shapes, and textures).

4. **Yin and Yang** (the balance of opposites around you).

5. **Continuity and Connectedness** (the link between what you see and what you attract).

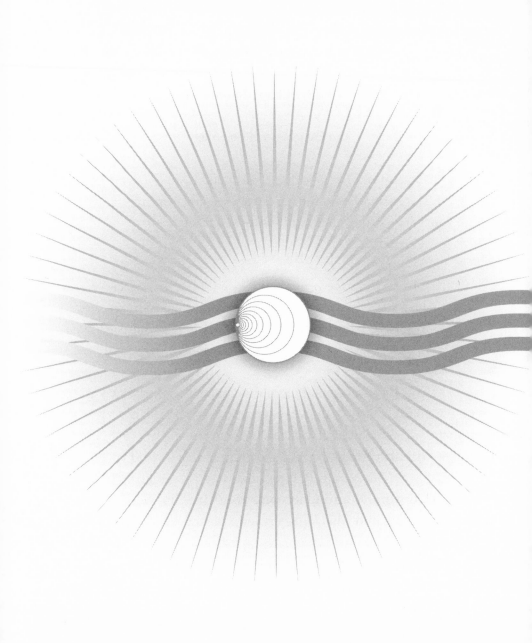

CHAPTER
4

POWER PRINCIPLE #1:
CHI

Don't buy the house; buy the neighborhood.
~Russian Proverb

Chi (pronounced *chee*) is the vital energy that comes from nature. It is the constantly moving and changing force around you, making you feel either good or bad in a certain location. Every person, object, and environment has the living energy we call chi. Chi is always in motion, swirling around people and around the objects that people place in their surroundings.

Outside, in nature, everything flows and moves like *wind and water*. However, in our indoor, built environment, we are all too often surrounded by sharp angles and straight lines or by objects placed in the locations that don't support what we want to attract. All of this can block the positive flow of chi energy.

In your home or office the chi will flow in through the front door and head straight out the first window or door in its path. The goal of Feng Shui adjustments is to stop the chi from rapidly leaving your space, and keep it flowing gently throughout every inch of your indoor environment, just like *wind and water*.

Chi can be either positive or negative. Consequently, it is often necessary to move objects or add new ones to bring about a change in the chi around you. Like Goldilocks, you instinctively know when the chi is not too strong, not too weak, but feels just right.

To better understand about *positive chi*, think about your favorite restaurant where you feel *at home* and linger over your meal. Can you remember the layout, colors, fabrics, the decoration on the walls, and the aromas that made you feel happy and welcome? Perhaps there are small tables arranged strategically to suggest intimacy, fresh cut flowers and candles on the tables, and inspiring artwork that transports you to the Italian countryside, all of which contributed to the positive chi that attracted you to the spot.

By contrast, think about an indoor space, such as an office, where you have felt uncomfortable. Remember the layout, colors, fabrics, decoration on the walls, and aromas to get a sense of what aspects created its negative chi. For example, there may have been stark white walls, angular metal desks, harsh fluorescent overhead lighting, split-pea-soup-colored carpet, and generic or no artwork, all making you feel alienated, unwelcome, and unhealthy. You watch the clock all day and can't wait to go home. That's how it feels to be in a location that has an overabundance of negative chi.

The Rule of 3Rs: Replace, Repair, Remove

In situations where chi gets stuck or blocked it can have extremely negative effects on your surroundings and on your everyday life. We call this negative condition *sha chi*. You can be emotionally, physically, and spiritually affected by the negative energy of *sha chi*.

When I conduct a Feng Shui analysis of a home or office, the first thing I do is look for the three major conditions of negative chi that are especially detrimental:

1. Things You Don't Like
2. Things That Are Broken
3. Things That Are Cluttered

Once I identify these negative conditions, I recommend ways to correct them following my *Rule of 3Rs*: Replace, Repair, or Remove all items creating negative chi as soon as possible.

Here are some examples of situations involving the three major conditions of negative chi, and how my clients used the *Rule of 3Rs* to fix them.

Negative Chi Condition #1: Things You Don't Like

SUCCESS STORY:
Sarah's Bedroom Furniture
Sarah hired me to conduct a home consultation because she was thinking about a career change. We

both quickly agreed about the one thing that was negative for Sarah: the bedroom set. Neither Sarah nor
her husband liked it, but Sarah's mother gave it to her
so she felt compelled to keep it or risk insulting her
mother. When I explained how it represented negative
chi for her, a whole new world of possibilities opened
up to Sarah. That night the couple went shopping and
found a new bedroom set they both adored, which was
delivered on Saturday. The next day Sarah opened up
the employment section of the Sunday paper and saw
a job that was perfect for her. She applied for — and
soon got — the job! The couple eventually donated
the old furniture to a refugee resettlement project,
which made them feel good about it for the first time.

If you have furniture, objects, artwork, and colors surrounding
you that you don't like or that have unhappy memories or feelings
attached to them, they reduce the positive chi in your environment
and create *sha chi*. I sometimes jokingly label this condition of
negative chi as "Aunt Bertha's Dresser." Let's say you inherited a
beautiful oak dresser from your mother's sister, your aunt Bertha.
You love your mom, but in all honesty you thought Aunt Bertha was
self-centered and acted like something that rhymed with the word
itch. But you put the dresser in your bedroom because it is valuable
and you want to keep the family peace. And after all, it was a gift
and she was your mom's favorite sibling.

Right?

Wrong!

When you furnish your home with objects that have negative emotions and attachments for you, you are living with all of their negative energy no matter how valuable they are. Therefore, if you have your own version of "Aunt Bertha's Dresser," I urge you to move it out of your home and get rid of all the negative chi that goes with it. Go through the rooms of your home with a pen and paper in hand and make an inventory of the objects and furniture you no longer like or that have negative associations. Then decide how you want to get rid of each object — either by donating, selling, or disposing of it — and replace it with something you truly love.

Negative Chi Condition #2: Things That Are Broken

SUCCESS STORY:

Angie and Jason's Front Porch Steps

Angie and Jason were having serious problems in their relationship, and some changes were badly needed. When Angie gave me directions to her historic Victorian, she cautioned me to come around to the back door because the crumbling front porch steps were too dangerous. My internal Feng Shui meter went into alert mode because the front door is called the mouth of chi where all of the good energy enters a home, and the area around it should always be kept in good repair. When I arrived, I found a board across the steps to prevent visitors from approaching the front door. The Feng Shui message was of *blockage* and *danger*. I saw the crumbling steps as a metaphor for the couple's crumbling marriage. I urged them to have the steps repaired quickly because the blocked entrance was symbolically blocking their lives. A few weeks later Angie e-mailed me that they finished the repairs to the steps. And more important, she and Jason had stopped quarreling.

Are you surrounded by things that are broken, ripped, torn, stained, dirty, in disrepair, or not working? These conditions represent a disregard for your home and, consequently, for yourself. Conditions like cracks, holes, chipped paint, peeling wallpaper, or dead plants represent negative forces in your life since they block the flow of positive energy around you. Leaks, especially, can result in a drain on your finances, since in Feng Shui water represents abundance.

When you fix what is broken or not working in your home, you will fix your life. I recommend you go through every room in your house to identify things that are leaking, clogged, burned out, broken, or stuck. Repair what you can immediately, then schedule dates to hire others to fix everything else.

Here are three quick fixes you can make where you will see an immediate, positive impact on your well-being:

1. If you have a broken mirror in your home, replace it, since it keeps you from seeing things clearly.

2. If a light bulb is burned out, change it, since it keeps you in the dark about your future.
3. If your kitchen faucet is leaking, fix it or call the plumber, since you are losing wealth and abundance.

Negative Chi Condition #3: Things That Are Cluttered

SUCCESS STORY:

Callie's Studio

Things were not going well for Callie at her stressful job with a nonprofit arts organization. She had previously offered private music lessons in her home studio but gave it up to take this job and let the studio become a clutter magnet. I advised her to start by cleaning up the home studio, since the clutter in this area made Callie's music seem unimportant. Within two days of starting her clutter clearing, something completely unexpected happened to Callie: in spite of glowing evaluations, she was asked to take a cut in pay and job title. She resigned on the spot. The next week she furiously cleared and cleaned her studio so she could begin giving music lessons again. Her private clients came back so quickly that she never saw a change in income. Within several months she was earning more than she ever imagined, with the added benefit of less stress and more time for her family.

In Feng Shui, clutter represents *postponed decisions* and the *inability to move forward*. Think about that for a while.

Where and why you have clutter says a lot about what is going on in your life. To improve positive energy flow and open up new possibilities for the future, I urge you to take a look at the reasons you have clutter in your home or office, then take steps to reduce it. I give you some specific steps for dealing with this critical aspect of improving positive energy flow in the "The Feng Shui Clutter Clinic" part of this book.

Poison Arrow Chi

Another type of negative chi is called "poison arrow chi." This occurs when two walls or sharp edges of objects come together and point out into a room, so that the chi acts like an arrow aimed at a target. When you sit in a room with a poison arrow, you become the target of its harsh energy. The chi around pointed edges can make the space uncomfortable or unhealthy, which in turn can have a negative effect on the quality of your sleep, health, relationships, job, or finances.

Besides walls, other examples of poison arrows inside a home or office include:

- the corner of a night table pointed at you in bed,

- the sharp edges of a bookcase aimed at you where you work,

- the sharp edges of an exposed ceiling beam pointed at you while you sleep,

- the knife-like edges of cabinets aimed at your neck in your kitchen,

- soffits, angular beams, and coffered or multilevel ceilings pointed at you, especially in your bedroom.

Examples of poison arrows outside a home or office include:

- the corner of another home or building pointed at your house,

- the edges of tall buildings blocking your view,

- massive objects like jagged rocks near your home,

- a tree planted directly in front of your door,

- a straight path or driveway leading up to your house,

- cell or radio towers aimed at or looming over your home,

- a neighbor's driveway pointing directly at your driveway,

- a T-junction, where two streets intersect and one street ends in front of your house.

Some poison arrows are more harmful than others. In general you need to be more concerned about fixing poison arrows coming at your house from outside than poison arrows inside your home. It is especially important to correct a T-junction, which in Feng Shui is called "tiger eyes." The headlights of cars coming down the street are like the penetrating eyes of a tiger piercing your home, making the energy harsh and uncomfortable.

Inside, the most troublesome poison arrows are those aimed at you in places where you spend long periods of time — for example, sleeping in your bed or working at a desk in your home or office — rather than cooking in the kitchen where you are constantly in motion.

Fixing Poison Arrows

Fixing exterior poison arrows aimed at your home is more difficult than making adjustments to correct interior ones where you usually have more control over changes. The cure for exterior poison arrows is to send the negative energy back to its source.

One simple way to do this is to place a convex, octagon-shaped mirror on the exterior of your home aimed at the offending object. Examples of this strategy can be seen in the Chinatown areas of cities like New York or San Francisco, where you will see mirrors called *bagua mirrors* above the doors of many buildings to deflect negative energy away from the structures.

If you can't hang a mirror above your door, or simply don't want to, you could place a reflective garden ornament between you and the offending structure to deflect the negative chi. Examples of these objects include a shiny gazing globe or metal sculpture.

The other option for dealing with poison arrows aimed at your home is to place an object that functions as a barrier between your house and the offending object. Such corrections include planting trees or tall shrubs or constructing a stone wall. You could also hang a wind chime to help deflect the negative chi away from your house.

If there is anything sharp aimed at your front door, such as the corner of a house, or anything large looming over your home, like a cell tower, or something blocking your house, like a telephone pole, it could symbolically limit opportunities and increase financial difficulties. Plant shrubs or trees between you and the offending object to protect your home from the impact of the poison arrow.

Inside corrections are a lot easier. If you are lucky enough to have the type of rounded, bull-nose corners that are prevalent in southwestern architecture, you have already avoided this problem; but for most homes, sharp corners are an issue that needs to be corrected.

The good news is that most poison arrows can be corrected by repositioning the furniture in front of the sharp edges so the poison arrow doesn't point at you. When you can't move the furniture, you can protect yourself from poison arrows by placing any kind of buffer between you and the sharp edge. This could be a potted or hanging plant, a piece of decorative fabric hung on the corner to soften it, or corner protectors attached to the shape edge to symbolically round it. A good way to deal with the poison arrows from coffered or multilevel ceilings is to hang fabric over the edge of the angular part of the ceiling, or drape sheer fabric over the bed like a canopy to simulate a false ceiling. If the edges of your night table point at you in bed, drape a cloth over the point. If a wall with a sharp point is aimed at your bed, place a plant or piece of furniture in front of it.

POWER PRINCIPLE #2:
THE FIVE ELEMENTS

When in doubt, wear red.
~ Bill Blass

*T*he *Five Elements* is the Feng Shui term to describe the colors, shapes, and textures around you and the attributes they bring into your life. This is the way you can use Feng Shui to color your world.

The Five Elements are: *Fire, Earth, Metal, Water,* and *Wood*. Each Element has a characteristic shape and colors and represents specific attributes. What do the names of the Five Elements conjure up in your mind? Most likely it is the same thing as their attributes: passion, grounding, clarity, movement, and growth, respectively.

The goal of Five Element theory is to use the actual material of the Element in your indoor environment to bring its power into your life. For example, a roaring fireplace adds the Fire Element to a room, a granite counter adds the Earth Element to your kitchen. But, when using the actual Element just isn't possible, you can use the colors or shape associated with it. The most powerful objects for making Feng Shui adjustments are those that combine the actual material, color, and shape of an Element.

Here is a description of each of the Five Elements and how to use them to power up your life:

▲ The Fire Element

Fire is the Element that represents passion, emotion, and high energy. The Fire Element is the reason why you never have a long, leisurely meal in a restaurant decorated in red, the ultimate Fire Element color. The color red is too full of energy to slow you down.

Actual Fire Element objects are hot and blazing, like burning candles or a roaring fireplace.

The colors of Fire are also hot, like red, crimson, scarlet, orange, deep purple, and pink. It's no accident that the fiery heroine in *Gone with the Wind* is named Scarlet.

The shape of the Fire Element is triangular, like a flame.

Quick Tip for Using the Fire Element

The color pink is associated with unconditional love and softness and with the innocence of youth. When you want to attract a new love into your life, surround yourself with pink.

The Earth Element

Earth is the Element that grounds you and makes you feel stable and balanced. That's why so many people love hardwood floors — the earthy color under your feet represents the Earth Element, which makes you feel grounded.

Actual Earth Element objects are composed of substances made from the earth, such as the tile floor in your bathroom, clay pots on your patio, and granite countertops in your kitchen. The soil in your potted plants is actual earth.

The colors of the Earth Element are the colors of your world: brown like the soil, yellow from the sun, terracotta like clay.

The shape of the Earth Element is square.

Quick Tip for Using the Earth Element

Yellow, the color of the sun, is associated with happiness, joy, and lifting your mood. If you are confused, anxious, fearful, or lack direction, add something yellow to your surroundings to balance and ground you.

The Metal Element

Metal is the Element that brings strength and clarity into your life. If you need to focus on a project, add a Metal object to your office.

Actual Metal Element objects are things like wrought iron furniture, a bronze light fixture, or a metal headboard. All electronics and computers are considered the Metal Element, as are fluorescent lights. If you work under fluorescent lighting all day and get headaches, it is because this Metal energy is *stabbing* you from overhead all day long.

The colors of the Metal Element are the metallic colors like gold and silver, plus all of the light colors like white, gray, and pastels.

The shape of the Metal Element is round, like a metal coin.

Quick Tip for Using the Metal Element

The color white is clean and represents innocence, flawlessness, and newness. When you want to start fresh on a project, surround yourself with white to represent a clean slate.

≋ The Water Element

Water is the Element that brings movement, flow, inspiration, and relaxation into your life. Think of the feeling you get watching a meandering river and you will understand the gentle power of the Water Element.

Actual Water Element objects are represented by an aquarium, fish bowl, or a fountain; symbolically, the Water Element is represented by glass and mirrors.

The colors of the Water Element are deep blues and black, as if you were looking into deep water.

The shape of the Water Element is anything that has a swirling or curving pattern, like a classic Oriental rug, a paisley print slipcover, or artwork that shows a river, lake, or the ocean.

Quick Tip for Using the Water Element

The color blue is soothing, calm, and relaxing. If you are stressed and need to relax, surround yourself with blue.

The Wood Element

Wood is the Element that represents growth, expansion, and vitality in your life. If your creativity is blocked, place a bushy green plant with rounded leaves on your desk to get your creative juices flowing.

Actual Wood Element objects are composed of natural wood, like wood furniture and hardwood floors, as well as plants and flowers.

The colors of the Wood Element are green and teal, like tree leaves.

The shape of the Wood Element is rectangular, somewhat like a tall, straight tree trunk.

Quick Tip for Using the Wood Element

Green is associated with growth, expansion, and unlimited horizons. If you feel stuck and need to make a decision, decorate your indoor environment with green plants.

Combining the Five Elements

The shapes and colors of an object can represent several Elements at once. To better understand this, try to visualize how all five of the Elements are represented by this coffee table: a round shape (Metal

Element shape) made from mahogany (Earth Element color and Wood Element composition) with a triangular inlaid red design (Fire Element color and shape) sitting on a black base (Water Element color).

The quick summary of the properties of the Five Elements displayed in table 5.1 can serve as a guide for using them to make Feng Shui adjustments in your home or office. Varying the colors on the wall and the shapes in a room, or changing the fabric color, art, photography, furniture, and decoration is the easiest way to bring the power of the Five Elements into any interior space.

Balancing the Elements

The goal of Feng Shui adjustments is to balance combinations of the Five Elements in your home or workplace. If there is too much or too little of one Element in your surroundings, things won't feel balanced and harmonious. Something about the room or space just won't feel right.

Certain Elements reduce or increase others through the process of the *Creation Cycle* and the *Destruction Cycle*. You can understand this interaction of Elements better if you think of a simple game of *rock-paper-scissors*: just as one object dominates another in the game, one Feng Shui Element triumphs over another in your interior surroundings.

For example, in the **Creation Cycle**, one particular Element *creates* another:

- Fire *creates* Earth (*yields ashes*)
- Earth *yields* Metal (*produces iron ore or crystals*)

Table 5.1 *The Five Elements*

Fire ▲	
Shape	Triangle
Colors	Red, Purple, Crimson, Magenta, Orange
Attributes	Passion, Emotion
Examples	Fireplace, Candles, Lights, Animal Prints, Cone-Shaped Objects
Too Little	Emotional Coldness
Too Much	Aggression, Impatience, Impulsiveness
Earth ■	
Shape	Square
Colors	Brown, Yellow, Terracotta
Attributes	Grounding, Stability, Order, Nourishment
Examples	Tile Floors, Ceramic Bowls, Clay Pots, Pebbles, Flat Objects
Too Little	Instability, Clutter, Chaos
Too Much	Heavy, Serious, Conservative
Metal ●	
Shape	Circle
Colors	White, Gray, Silver, Gold, Pastels
Attributes	Strength, Focus, Clarity, Precision
Examples	Metal Furniture, Computers, Fluorescent Lights, Mounded Objects
Too Little	Indecisiveness, Procrastination, Confusion
Too Much	Mental Rigidity, Stubbornness, Inability to Compromise
Water ≋	
Shape	Curvy or Patterned
Colors	Deep Blue, Black
Attributes	Relaxation, Inspiration, Movement
Examples	Mirrors, Glass, Fish Tanks, Fountains, Patterned Objects
Too Little	Stress, Rivalry, Anxiety
Too Much	Reduced Productivity, Spaciness
Wood ■	
Shape	Rectangle
Colors	Green, Teal
Attributes	Growth, Expansion, Vitality
Examples	Plants, Flowers, Forest Scenes, Wood Furniture, Textiles, Columns
Too Little	Stagnation, Blocked Creativity and Intuition
Too Much	Overwhelmed, Overcommitted

- Metal *attracts* Water (*forms condensation*)
- Water *feeds* Wood (*grows it*)
- Wood *fuels* Fire (*keeps it burning*)

On the other hand, in the **Destruction Cycle**, one Element *overpowers* another:

- Fire *consumes* Wood (*destroys it*)
- Earth *contains* Fire (*stops it from burning*)
- Metal *cuts* Earth (*removes it*)
- Water *rusts* Metal (*corrodes it*)
- Wood *drinks* Water (*uses it up*)

The good thing about these cycles is that when you use them to symbolically *create* or *destroy* Elements, you get to keep your flaming red sofa (Fire Element) in an area of your home that would be better off having a blue one (Water Element). To create balance in the room, you would add something brown (Earth Element) to symbolically smother some of the Fire from your sofa and let the Water predominate.

Where are the Five Elements located in the rooms of your home? I recommend you go through each room and make a list of the objects that represent each Element, keeping in mind that an Element can be represented by the actual material, its shape, or its color.

If you have too little of one Element in a room, or an excess of another, you can use the Creation or Destruction Cycle to decide which objects and colors you need to add to create balance. The reference chart in table 5.2 will help in using the formulas for enhancing or diminishing the power of the Elements. This process

Table 5.2 *Balancing the Five Elements*

If You Have...	Add...
FIRE ▲	
Too *Little*	Wood ▮ (fuels Fire)
Too **Much**	Earth ▦ (contains Fire) *or* Water ≈ (drowns Fire)
EARTH ▦	
Too *Little*	Fire ▲ (creates Earth)
Too **Much**	Metal ● (digs Earth) *or* Wood ▮ (contains Earth)
METAL ●	
Too *Little*	Earth ▦ (yields Metal)
Too **Much**	Water ≈ (rusts Metal) *or* Fire ▲ (melts Metal)
WATER ≈	
Too *Little*	Metal ● (sweats Water)
Too **Much**	Wood ▮ (drinks Water) *or* Earth ▦ (absorbs Water)
WOOD ▮	
Too *Little*	Water ≈ (feeds Wood)
Too **Much**	Fire ▲ (consumes Wood) *or* Metal ● (cuts Wood)

lets you use the power of Feng Shui, while you get to keep the objects that you love.

Have Fun with the Elements

Ready to have some fun with the Five Elements? Take the *Elemental Personality Quiz* to see which is your dominant Element. Is the Element you are most drawn to the same one you are already using to decorate your home or office?

ELEMENTAL PERSONALITY QUIZ

Which color(s) do you most prefer?
 a. reds or purples
 b. shades of brown
 c. grays and reflective colors
 d. blues or black
 e. greens

Which personality trait describes you best?
 a. funny
 b. easy-going
 c. analytical
 d. creative
 e. driven

How would you describe your most recent romantic relationship ?
 a. passionate
 b. stable
 c. on again/off again
 d. private
 e. dramatic

Which tendency needs the most work in your life?
 a. irresponsibility
 b. worry
 c. inhibition
 d. suspicion
 e. anger

Which design choice sounds most appealing?
 a. artsy and eclectic
 b. comfortable and cozy
 c. smooth, clean and minimalist
 d. peaceful and healing
 e. garden-like or floral

How would you most likely approach a problem?
 a. optimistically
 b. carefully
 c. systematically
 d. creatively
 e. aggressively

Which of the following do you value most?
 a. fame and reputation
 b. knowledge
 c. travel
 d. career
 e. community

Which activity would you prefer?
 a. entertaining at a fabulous party
 b. gardening and landscaping
 c. traveling with friends to a favorite city
 d. swimming or lounging near water
 e. hiking or camping in a forest

What would you recommend to a friend in crisis?
 a. think clearly, take control
 b. get grounded before taking action
 c. find the good in this situation
 d. look within to find the solution
 e. make a fresh start

Which cause would you most likely support?
 a. boosting the arts
 b. a campaign for social justice
 c. improving the quality of education
 d. spiritual/religious ideals
 e. environmental protection

ANSWER KEY:

If you answered with mostly…

a: You could have a **Fire** dominated personality. You are quick-thinking, passionate, friendly, and impulsive. You have a playful side that can be downright naughty at times. Those who are too fiery have tendencies to be loud and critical. Smother your flames a bit by adding Earth Elements to bring balance.

b: You seem to have an abundance of **Earth** in your life. You are nurturing, stable, honest, and diplomatic. You are reliable though sometimes overly so. Too much earthiness can keep you from making desirable changes in your life. Add Metal Elements to brighten your prospects.

c: **Metal** Elements are prevalent in your nature. You are focused, disciplined, ethical, and eloquent. You value precision but might have a tendency to be overly critical at times. Highly metallic personalities might construct solid boundaries around themselves that even loved ones will have trouble penetrating. Allow flowing Water Elements to soften your hard exterior.

d: **Water** Elements figure highly in your character. You are creative, contemplative, patient, and self-aware. You feel things deeply and tend, at times, to internalize these feelings. Very watery people are easily overwhelmed and have trouble making decisions. Invite Wood Elements into your life to absorb your fluid emotions.

e: Your disposition could be ruled by **Wood** energy. Woodsy folks are confident, ambitious, determined, and compassionate. You work hard but sometimes too hard. An abundance of Wood can cause you to push yourself and others past a reasonable limit. Add some playful Fire Elements to help you take life less seriously.

Evenly: You are well–balanced. All Five Elements seem to be working in harmony in your life. You have good Feng Shui!

Quiz reprinted from "Feng Shui — A Functional Art," *Hagerstown Magazine*, Hagerstown, Maryland.

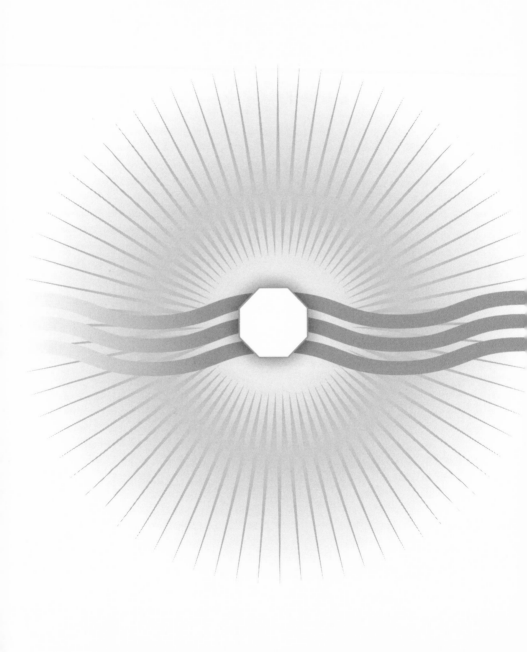

POWER PRINCIPLE #3:
THE BAGUA

What I dream of is an art of balance.
~Henry Matisse

*N*ow that you are familiar with the Feng Shui Elements, you can decide where to place them, in the form of furniture, objects, art, and paint colors, in your home or office. The map used to place Elements is called a bagua (pronounced *bag-wha*), a word that means eight-sided in Chinese. The traditional Feng Shui bagua is an octagon that contains eight areas plus a grounding center, for a total of nine areas or *guas*, corresponding to critical aspects of daily life.

The bagua is a fundamental tool of Feng Shui. You use it to determine which part of a home or office relates to a specific aspect of life, such as wealth, harmony, and love. Understanding how to use a bagua is a basic step in making Feng Shui adjustments.

Here are the nine areas of the Feng Shui bagua:

- Power/Wealth/Abundance
- Fame/Future/Reputation
- Love/Marriage/Relationships
- Creativity/Children/Legacy
- Compassion/Travel/Helpful People
- Self/Career/Work
- Knowledge/Wisdom/Harmony
- Family/Health/Community
- Well-Being/Balance

Contemporary approaches to Feng Shui use a grid-shaped chart instead of an octagon. The grid-shaped bagua contains the same eight life areas and grounding center as the traditional octagon-shaped map, but most people relate better to a rectangle because we tend to live in rectangular- or square-shaped homes and work in rectangular or square offices. In addition, according to Feng Shui principles, the most auspicious shape for a home or building is like a box — square or rectangle — since these shapes allow equal division for each *gua*, or bagua area, when using the mapping chart. So using a grid-shaped bagua map just seems to make more sense in our contemporary world.

No matter what shape house you live in or office space you work in, the bagua chart is always oriented from the front door or main entrance, looking into the home or room to be mapped.

Understanding the Bagua

To get started, familiarize yourself with what a contemporary bagua looks like. There are two versions of the same bagua on the following pages: a vertical version and a horizontal version.

- Use the **vertical** shape (figure 6.1) if the floor plan, or *footprint*, of your home is longer front to back than it is side to side, such as a townhouse or row house.

- Use the **horizontal** bagua (figure 6.2) if the shape of the floor plan of your home is wider from side to side than it is from front to back, like a colonial, split level, rambler, or ranch style house.

You can download color PDF versions of the vertical or horizontal bagua from my website: *http://www.fengshuiforreallife.com/basics*.

The Nine Areas of the Bagua

I am often asked why the bagua areas represent what they do. The simple answer is that when we orient the bagua from the way we enter a space, the location of each of the nine areas reflects our life experience.

First, when we enter a building or room, the things we aspire to in life — **wealth/power**, **fame/recognition**, **love/marriage** — are always the furthest away from us, on the opposite side of the room. We move toward these goals as we move into a space.

Figure 6.1 *Vertical Bagua*

POWER • WEALTH ABUNDANCE Generate Cash Flow Raise Money Increase Prosperity Fire Red • Purple ▲	**FAME • FUTURE REPUTATION** Increase Recognition Establish Reputation Become Well Known Fire Red • Orange ▲	**LOVE • MARRIAGE RELATIONSHIPS** Attract Love Enhance Relationship Improve Self-Esteem Fire Red • Pink ▲
FAMILY • HEALTH COMMUNITY Cultivate Social Life Strengthen Family Ties Improve Health Wood Green ■	**WELL-BEING BALANCE** Achieve Balance Recover From Illness Increase Athletic Abilities Earth Yellow • Brown ■	**CREATIVITY CHILDREN • LEGACY** Unblock Creativity Start New Project Connect with Children Metal White • Gray • Metallic ●
KNOWLEDGE WISDOM • HARMONY Attend School or Study Encourage Self-Growth Cultivate Peaceful Life Water Blue • Black ≋	**SELF • CAREER WORK** Change Jobs Switch Career Fields Meet New Work Goals Water Blue • Black ≋	**COMPASSION • TRAVEL HELPFUL PEOPLE** Attract Clients or Mentors Travel or Relocate Strengthen Spirituality Metal White • Gray • Metallic ●

ORIENT WITH PRIMARY ENTRANCE ALONG THIS LINE

Figure 6.2 *Horizontal Bagua*

POWER • WEALTH ABUNDANCE	FAME • FUTURE REPUTATION	LOVE • MARRIAGE RELATIONSHIPS
Generate Cash Flow Increase Prosperity **Fire** **Red • Purple** ▲	Increase Recognition Become Well Known **Fire** **Red • Orange** ▲	Attract Love Improve Self-Esteem **Fire** **Red • Pink** ▲
FAMILY • HEALTH COMMUNITY	WELL-BEING BALANCE	CREATIVITY CHILDREN • LEGACY
Cultivate Social Life Improve Health & Family Ties **Wood** **Green** ■	Recover From Illness Increase Athletic Abilities **Earth** **Yellow • Brown** ■	Unblock Creativity Connect with Children **Metal** **White • Gray • Metallic** ●
KNOWLEDGE WISDOM • HARMONY	SELF • CAREER WORK	COMPASSION • TRAVEL HELPFUL PEOPLE
Encourage Self-Growth Cultivate Peaceful Life **Water** **Blue • Black** ≋	Switch Career Fields Meet New Work Goals **Water** **Blue • Black** ≋	Attract Clients or Mentors Travel or Relocate **Metal** **White • Gray • Metallic** ●

ORIENT WITH PRIMARY ENTRANCE ALONG THIS LINE

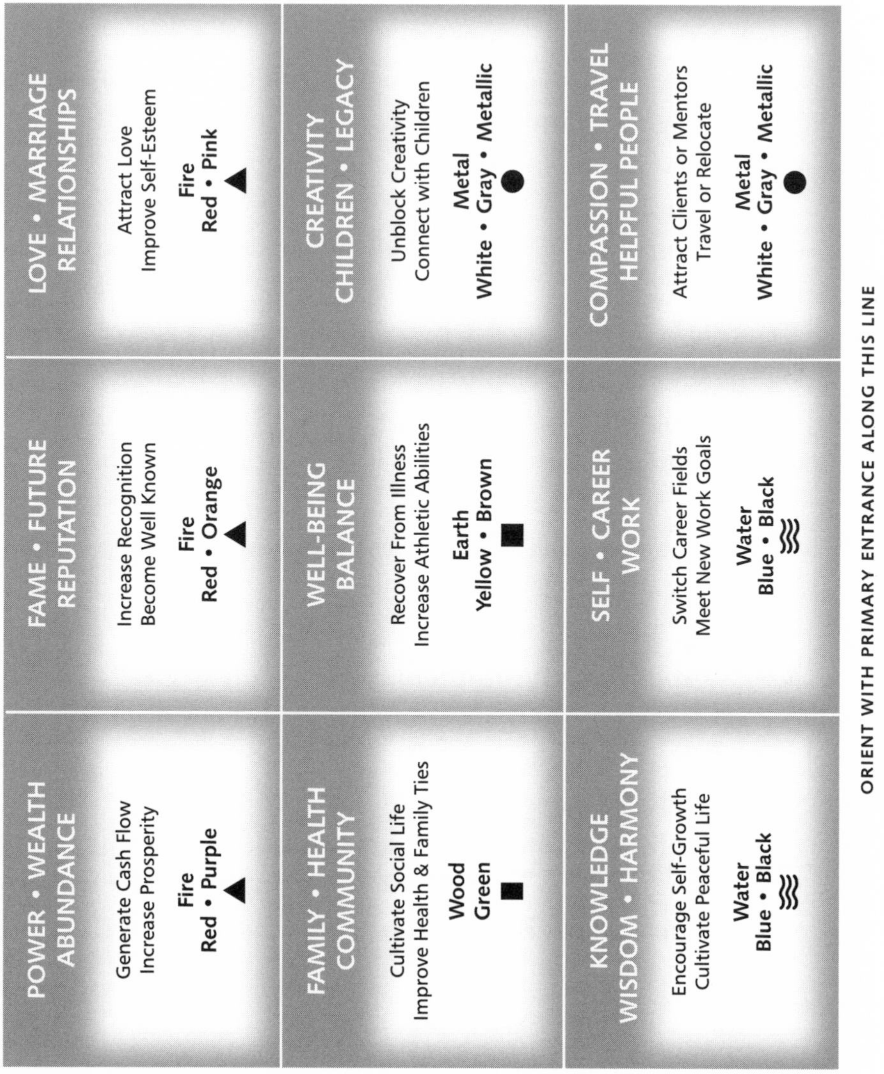

The **self/career** area, which represents the journey or path that our life is on and our specific life's work, is in the center bottom of the room.

The people and things that help us reach our goals, known as the **knowledge/wisdom** and **compassion/helpful people**, flank our life's work, providing a solid base for our progress.

As you move further into a space, **family/community** and **children/creativity** surround us on either side, accompanying us on our journey.

The center of any home is its **grounding** area, since everything around us relates to our ability to be comfortably balanced in our space.

To make things *happen* in your life, you need to activate, enhance, and rev up the particular area of the bagua that relates to the part of your life that needs a bit of help.

Here are the bagua areas again, and a description of the aspects of life to which they relate:

- **Power/Wealth/Abundance** — *Enhance this area if you want to...*
  - Generate cash flow
  - Raise money
  - Increase prosperity and abundance

- **Fame/Future/Reputation** — *Enhance this area if you want to...*
  - Increase recognition
  - Establish a good reputation
  - Become well known

- **Love/Marriage/Relationships** — *Enhance this area if you want to...*
  - Attract love
  - Improve existing relationship
  - Improve self-esteem

- **Creativity/Children/Legacy** — *Enhance this area if you want to...*
  - Unblock creativity
  - Start a new project
  - Improve relationships with children

- **Compassion/Travel/Helpful People** — *Enhance this area if you want to...*
  - Attract clients and mentors
  - Increase travel or relocate
  - Strengthen spirituality

- **Self/Career/Work** — *Enhance this area if you want to...*
  - Change your job
  - Switch career fields
  - Meet new work goals

- **Knowledge/Wisdom/Harmony** — *Enhance this area if you want to...*
  - Attend school or study
  - Encourage self-growth
  - Cultivate a peaceful life

- **Family/Health/Community** — *Enhance this area if you want to...*
  - Cultivate your social life
  - Strengthen family ties
  - Improve your health

- **Well-Being/Balance** — *Enhance this area if you want to...*
  - Achieve balance
  - Recover from illness
  - Increase athletic abilities

Using the Bagua

Now that you have picked the bagua that most closely matches the shape of your house, you can begin to use it to map your home.

Step 1: Draw Your Floor Plan

Draw the floor plan of the first floor of your home. For this exercise, I recommend you work with only the first floor, but ultimately you will want to draw the floor plan for each floor of your home, including the basement and attic levels if you have them.

Be sure to include all areas and attached structures, such as the garage, side porch, and deck. In Feng Shui these are considered "real rooms" and need to be included in the floor plan sketch. Everything that is connected to your first floor should appear in your floor plan sketch.

Figure 6.3 *Floor plan for the first floor of an L-shaped house*

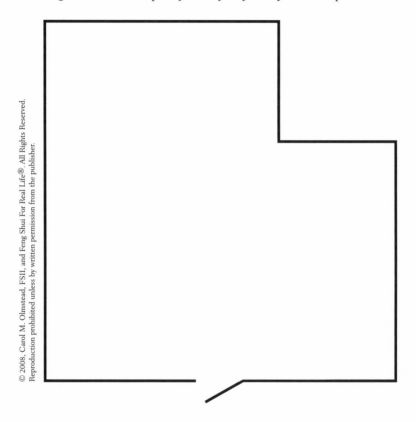

Figure 6.3 illustrates an example of a floor plan for the first floor of a simple L-shaped home.

Step 2: Orient the Bagua from the Front Door

Whichever bagua map you choose based on the shape of your home, orient it by standing at your front door looking in to your home and holding the map in front of you.

The front door is called "the mouth of chi" because this is the way the architect or builder designed your home to be entered, and the positive chi also enters your home through this door. Even if you usually enter your home through the garage, back porch, mud room, or side door, you will still orient the bagua from the true front door.

Step 3: Superimpose the Bagua Map over Your Floor Plan

Divide the floor plan of your home into the nine equal bagua areas:
- Power/Wealth/Abundance
- Fame/Future/Reputation
- Love/Relationship/Marriage
- Creativity/Children/Legacy
- Compassion/Travel/Helpful People
- Self/Career/Work
- Knowledge/Wisdom/Harmony
- Family/Health/Community
- Well-Being/Balance

Figure 6.4 shows the floor plan of our sample house divided into the nine areas of the bagua. For now, disregard the one area of the bagua that lies outside the walls of the home. I will show you how to fix that later in this chapter.

Once you have divided your home into the nine bagua areas, take a look at your drawing to see where the rooms lie within the bagua.

Figure 6.4 *My floor plan divided into the nine areas of the bagua*

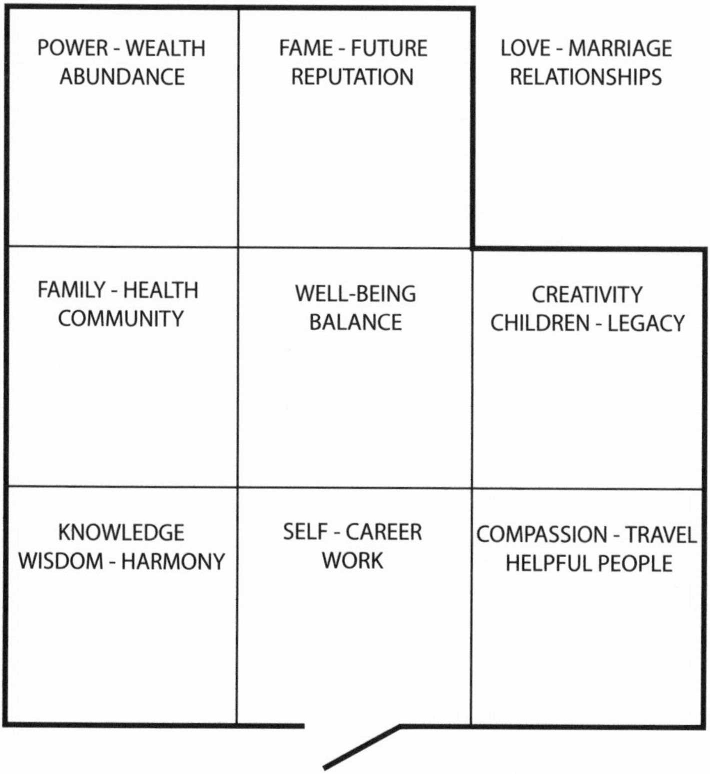

POWER - WEALTH ABUNDANCE	FAME - FUTURE REPUTATION	LOVE - MARRIAGE RELATIONSHIPS
FAMILY - HEALTH COMMUNITY	WELL-BEING BALANCE	CREATIVITY CHILDREN - LEGACY
KNOWLEDGE WISDOM - HARMONY	SELF - CAREER WORK	COMPASSION - TRAVEL HELPFUL PEOPLE

For example, is your living room located in the Wealth/Abundance area? If so, this is the perfect placement because this bagua area should be decorated with valuable objects and collections, something most of us instinctively put in our living rooms.

Is your bathroom located in the Well-Being/Grounding area of your home? This is not such good placement because you could be symbolically flushing your well-being down the toilet. Some Feng

Shui corrections are necessary to stop the drain and can be accomplished by adding the Earth Element.

In figure 6.5, you can see that in our sample house, the family room is located in the Fame/Future/Recognition area. This is a terrific Feng Shui location for a room where the family gathers because you can display items like the trophies, diplomas, certificates, and sports awards the members of your family have received to activate this area.

Step 4: Decorate Your Rooms

Once you know what each area of your home represents, you can add furniture, accessories, and colors that represent the appropriate Elements to activate these areas.

Here are some suggestions for the types of objects to place in each bagua area to activate its attributes and qualities:

- **Power/Wealth/Abundance:**
    - Valuable possessions and collections, such as coins
    - Expensive art and antiques
    - Pictures of desired objects, like homes, jewelry, cars
    - Plants and flowers or images of plants and growing things
    - Triangular objects
    - Red, purple, dark blue objects

- **Fame/Future/Reputation:**
    - Diplomas, awards, prizes

Figure 6.5 *The location of Fame/Future/Recognition area in my home*

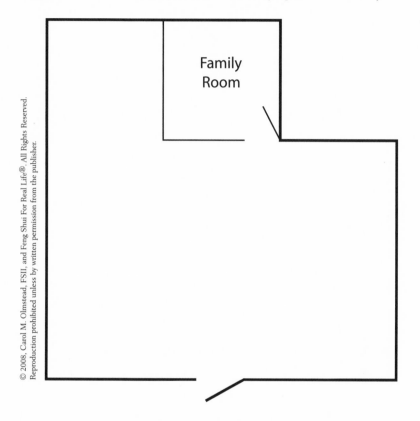

- Pictures that represent what you want to achieve in the future
- Images of a sunrise
- Things made from leather, wool, feathers
- Triangular objects
- Red objects

- **Love/Relationships/Marriage:**
    - Photos of you and your spouse/partner
    - Pairs of objects, like hearts, doves, cranes
    - Pictures of romantic images and places
    - Objects that represent love and marriage for you
    - Triangular objects
    - Red, pink, white objects

- **Creativity/Children/Legacy:**
    - Artwork and pictures that show children
    - Whimsical images and images you associate with childhood
    - Creative projects, craft supplies, hobbies
    - Things that you associate with creativity
    - Round objects
    - White, pastel, or metallic objects

- **Compassion/Travel/Helpful People:**
    - Images or items that represent mentors and heroes
    - Successful business projects
    - Religious or spiritual objects
    - Pictures of places you want to visit
    - Round or oval objects
    - Gray, white, or metallic objects

- **Self/Career/Work:**
    - Water features, fountains and fish tanks
    - Artwork depicting rivers, lakes, waterfalls, oceans

- Crystal or glass objects and mirrors
- Items that represent career success to you
- Flowing and freeform objects
- Black and dark blue objects

- **Knowledge/Wisdom/Harmony:**
    - Books, DVDs, CDs, Tapes
    - School materials and things being studied
    - Artwork depicting mountains or images of wise people
    - Images that represent peace and harmony for you
    - Flowing and freeform objects
    - Deep blue and black objects

- **Family/Health/Community:**
    - Photos and artwork of family groups, relatives, friends
    - Heirlooms and valuable antiques
    - Flowers and pictures of flowers and gardens
    - Items you associate with family and good health
    - Rectangular objects
    - Green and wood objects

- **Well-Being/Balance:**
    - Artwork that depicts mountains
    - Ceramic and clay objects
    - Objects that make you feel grounded, stable, and secure
    - Items you associate with well-being
    - Square objects
    - Brown, yellow, and terracotta objects

When adding objects, shapes, or colors to activate a bagua area, some people are tempted to overdue it and put all of these items in each of the bagua areas of their home. I recommend you resist the urge to over-adjust. One or two items that represent the attributes of each bagua area for you will do the job.

Arranging and Decorating Your Rooms

You can use the bagua as a guide for arranging and decorating each room as well as for the whole house.

First, stand at the front door looking into the home holding the bagua map in front of you to determine which room is in each bagua area of your home. Next, stand at the doorway to each room and hold the bagua in front of you. Then map out that room to see where the furniture and objects are best located.

For example, when you map your kitchen, are the knives stored in the Love/Relationship area of that room? If so, they could be symbolically "cutting" your relationships and need to be relocated.

You can also use the map to determine where to place things on any surface, such as your desk. For example, if you want to make your phone ring more with business from customers and clients, move it into the wealth corner of your desk.

To better understand how to arrange objects in a room, look at figure 6.6, which shows the family room of our simple home with the bagua map superimposed over the arrangement of furniture.

The following are some objects we can place in each bagua area of our sample family room to activate its corresponding energy:

Figure 6.6 *The bagua map superimposed over the arrangement of furniture in our family room*

- **Power/Wealth/Abundance:** Display a crystal bowl or valuable antique on the table to represent current and future prosperity.

- **Fame/Future/Reputation:** Hang artwork showing a vivid red sunrise to symbolize a bright future.

- **Love/Marriage/Relationships:** Place two red placemats and a pair of candles on the table to create a romantic space to share a glass of wine.

- **Children/Creativity/Legacy:** Keep your CDs and DVDs here to gather the family to watch videos or listen to music together.

- **Compassion/Travel/Helpful People:** Hang artwork showing a mentor or hero who influenced you, whether it's Mother Theresa, or Albert Einstein, or Tiger Woods.

- **Self/Career/Work:** Place a plant and nurture it to represent a constantly growing and expanding career.

- **Knowledge/Wisdom/Harmony:** Place the books you are reading on the table to symbolize wisdom and peace in your life.

- **Family/Health/Community:** Sit in a curved sofa and chairs to create a comfortable, *wind-water* place for the family to gather and share.

- **Well-Being/Balance:** Place a square rug in the center of the room to make everyone feel grounded and secure in the room.

Figure 6.7 *The missing bagua area in our home*

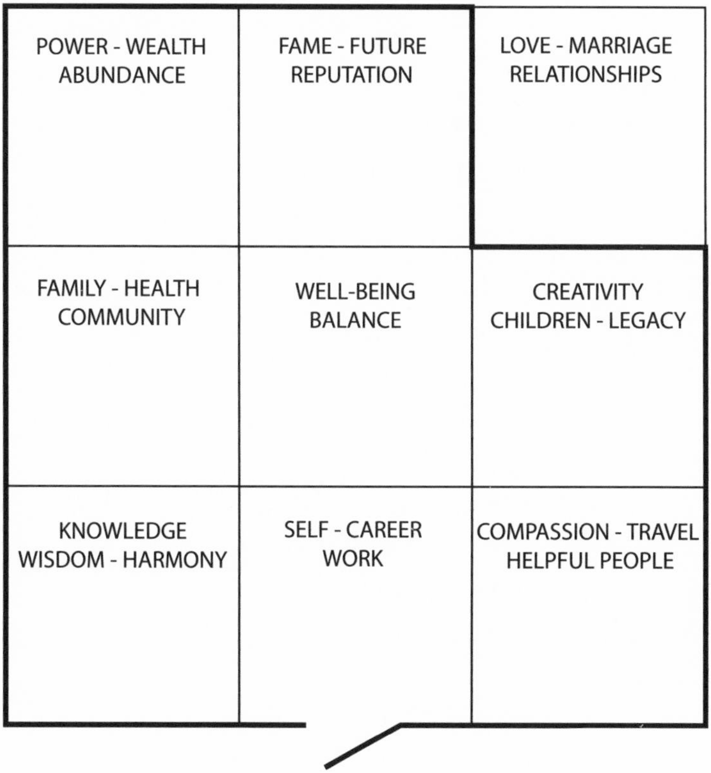

POWER - WEALTH ABUNDANCE	FAME - FUTURE REPUTATION	LOVE - MARRIAGE RELATIONSHIPS
FAMILY - HEALTH COMMUNITY	WELL-BEING BALANCE	CREATIVITY CHILDREN - LEGACY
KNOWLEDGE WISDOM - HARMONY	SELF - CAREER WORK	COMPASSION - TRAVEL HELPFUL PEOPLE

Correcting Missing Bagua Areas

Many architects today are creating architectural wonders that can sometimes cause unfortunate Feng Shui disasters for the people who have to live in them because they are missing critical areas of the bagua. When a house is missing bagua areas, its occupants are missing the corresponding attributes from their lives.

In Feng Shui the most auspicious shape for a house or other building is like a box — a square or a rectangle — but in the real world people usually live in irregular-shaped structures. Or, even if they start out in a rectangular house, they may have remodeled and changed the shape by adding a room, deck, or covered porch, thus eliminating a critical bagua area.

For example, as figure 6.7 illustrates, by its design, our sample home is missing a crucial bagua area, the Love/Marriage/Relationship area.

This could mean that a couple living in this house might have a rocky relationship or have to work very hard to keep their love alive. In either case, they could benefit from making some Feng Shui changes to correct the bagua and the imbalance that is contributing to their relationship problems.

Whenever there are bagua areas outside the physical structure of your house, apartment, or office, you can simply complete, or *anchor*, the missing area in order to bring back the missing attribute. Fortunately, Feng Shui offers an easy and straightforward means to correct missing bagua areas.

First, you square off the missing vertical and horizontal lines to symbolically *complete* the missing areas of the home. This involves finding the point outside where the walls of the house would have come together *if* it were a complete square or rectangle. Then, you mark this spot in a symbolic way. This location might be in the backyard, front yard, in the alley, or on the driveway.

For example, figure 6.8 displays the floor plan of our sample house, which has been divided into the nine bagua areas, with an X marking the spot where the walls would have come together if this house were a complete square.

Figure 6.8 *X marks the spot where the walls would have come together if this house were a complete square.*

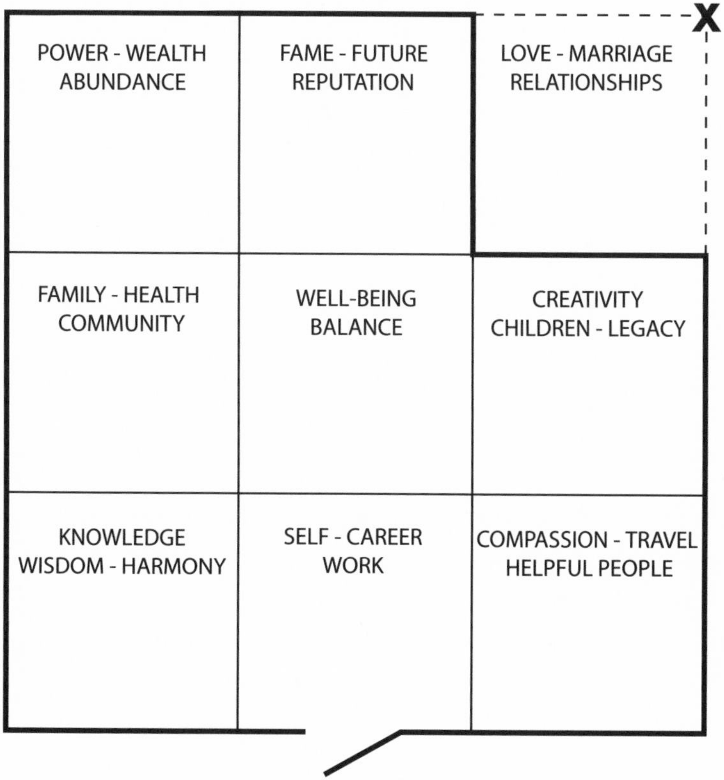

POWER - WEALTH ABUNDANCE	FAME - FUTURE REPUTATION	LOVE - MARRIAGE RELATIONSHIPS
FAMILY - HEALTH COMMUNITY	WELL-BEING BALANCE	CREATIVITY CHILDREN - LEGACY
KNOWLEDGE WISDOM - HARMONY	SELF - CAREER WORK	COMPASSION - TRAVEL HELPFUL PEOPLE

Second, you place an object, called a correction or cure, at this point to symbolically anchor the house and return the missing area into your home — and back into your life. When the point of correction falls on a hard surface like a path, sidewalk, or driveway, you can paint a small design to mark the spot. The more the design relates to the Elements and attributes of the missing bagua area, the better. The correction you place outside of the main level of your home will anchor the entire home, and it is not necessary to make any further adjustments on the different levels to correct the shape of your home.

X Marks the Spot

The object you select to anchor the house can be as simple as a meaningful stone, a bush, a colorful planter with flowers, a wind chime, or a bird feeder.

However, the more the object you select for the correction relates to the attributes of the missing bagua area (like Love/Marriage in our sample house), and the more it relates to the Element that belongs in that area (the Fire Element in our sample house), the more effective your cure will be. In our sample house, one good correction might be to place a bistro table and two chairs in the backyard at the critical spot.

As in our sample house, the Love/Relationship area is frequently missing from a home because of the shape created by a porch or deck. Another area that is frequently missing is the Helpful People/Compassion/Spirituality area, this time because of the placement of the garage. Some of my clients have placed corrections related to their spiritual beliefs in this area, including a statue of St. Francis or Buddha, or a garden tile with a Jewish star.

To better illustrate how you can correct for a missing bagua area, this story describes how I helped a client successfully anchor her missing Love/Relationship area.

Laura's Missing Love Area

When I walked into Laura's L-shaped home it was obvious that the Love/Relationship area was missing. Divorced for more than twelve years, Laura was more than ready for a new relationship, but it wasn't happening for her. I explained how the missing area related to the love that was missing in her life. Then I helped her mark the missing corner of her house with a pair of red ceramic flower pots that she had been storing in the basement and urged her to plant red geraniums in them. Some time later, I received this e-mail from Laura:

What an eye-opener when you said I was missing the Love/Relationship area of my house. I couldn't stop telling people about it, and how it was the perfect metaphor for what was going on in my life. I quickly added red flowers to the planters to help anchor the love area and bring love back into my life. Almost immediately after that I met Mike. Really, I couldn't believe it! He is a wonderful man and we have been together for more than a year now. Thank you for this eye-opening explanation of the missing area in my house. Mike and I will call you when we start looking for a new house together.

Figure 6.9 *Complex floor plan missing more than one bagua area*

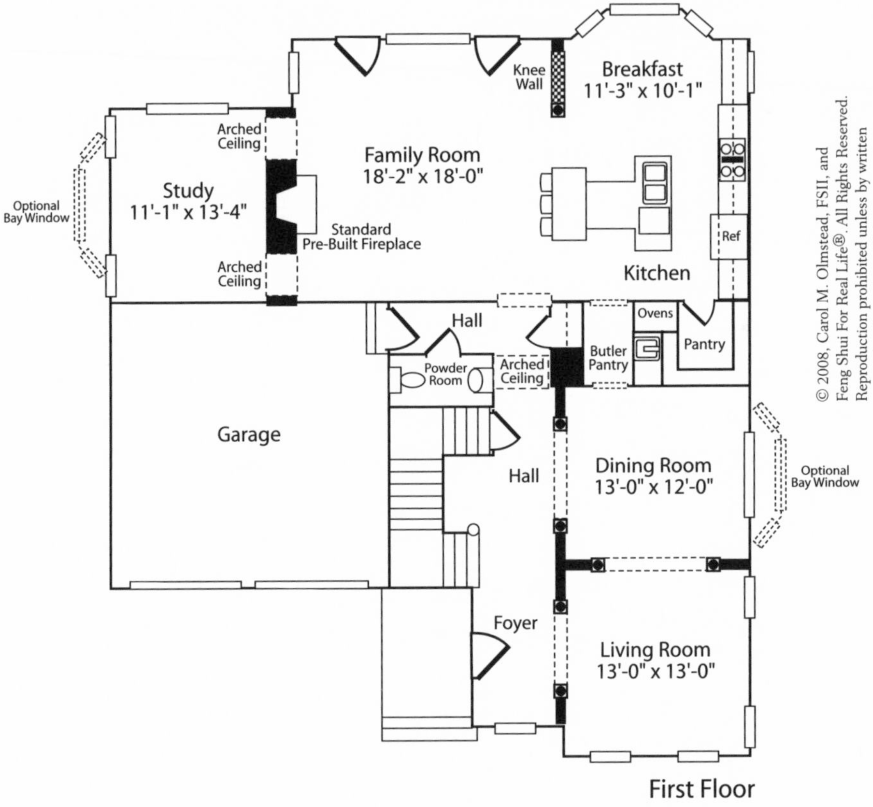

First Floor

When There's More Than One

Many of our homes are missing more than one bagua area. To understand how to correct a house that is missing several areas, use the bagua map to divide the more complex floor plan in figure

6.9, and determine where you need to place cures to correct for the missing areas of the house.

Once you have learned how to make corrections on floor plans of other people's homes, the next step is to find and correct all of the missing bagua areas in your own house so that you can anchor them with appropriate objects. Grab a sheet of graph paper, draw your own floor plan, and place Xs on your diagram where you need to make any corrections to complete the bagua. Then decide what objects to use to anchor any missing areas, and place your correction at the spot or spots marked on your diagram.

After you have used the bagua to correct for missing areas of your home, you can map each room to determine where to place the furniture, objects, and colors to balance various Elements.

Because Feng Shui adjustments can be fun, it can be easy to get carried away. But I recommend you resist the urge to overdo. When you make a lot of changes at once, the effect can be overwhelming. Make a few changes and add a few things, then step back and watch what happens to the energy in your home or office before you make more adjustments.

Adjustments for Apartments and Offices

Correcting for missing bagua areas in apartments, condos, and offices presents a different set of challenges from those of houses. It is usually not possible to make corrections outside of these spaces because a missing bagua area might be in the middle of your neighbor's living room or your colleague's office.

Adjustments for apartments and offices involve hanging appropriate objects on the wall adjacent to the missing area to symbolically *move* the wall and bring the missing bagua area back into your own space. Two types of objects work to symbolically move walls: mirrors, and art that depicts the natural world that is living and growing outside of our walls.

When you hang a mirror on the wall you no longer see the wall, but rather, you see what the mirror reflects. In essence you are seeing through the wall and therefore moving it symbolically.

Similarly, when you hang what I generically call *landscape artwork* — images of trees, flowers, meadows, rivers, mountains, and all the living, growing things you see in nature — you no longer see a wall, but the image of the outdoors.

Pick the wall you want to push out based on the bagua map, hang either a mirror or landscape or natural art on it, and you will achieve similar results to marking the outside spot. While actually marking the spot outside your home is the preferred way to correct a missing bagua, symbolically moving a wall can also be an effective way to make this adjustment.

CHAPTER

7

POWER PRINCIPLE #4:

YIN & YANG

His house was perfect, whether you liked food, or sleep, or work,
or story telling, or singing, or just sitting and thinking, best,
or a pleasant mixture of them all.
~ J. R. R. Tolkien

eng Shui aims to achieve a balance of the opposing characteristics in the world around you, which are known as *yin* and *yang*. You are probably familiar with the universal symbol for yin and yang: a circle with a curved line in the middle that divides the black and white halves of the circle, with a spot of each opposite color on the opposite side.

According to the yin-yang theory, everything in the universe consists of two opposing, but interconnected, forces: *yin*, which is feminine, and *yang*, which is masculine. Yin qualities are *female — soft, passive, nurturing, dark* — while the yang qualities are *male — hard, active, aggressive, bright.*

Yin and yang are the everyday opposites we see around us in our homes and offices: soft and hard, cold and hot, dark and light. Yin and yang exist in nature, in buildings, and in individual rooms. According to Feng Shui principles, it is the appropriate interaction of these two forces that creates harmony around us.

Yin-yang theory is another way that you can use Feng Shui to balance your interior surroundings. For example, if you paint a room a dark color, keep it cold, keep your children and pets out of it and rarely use it, it becomes yin. However, if you paint the same room a light color, turn up the temperature, and invite your friends, neighbors, and pets to join you in using it, it becomes yang.

In most cases we balance yin and yang naturally and instinctively in our homes: we add soft seat cushions to hard wooden chairs; if the bathwater gets too hot, we turn on the cold; we paint one wall a darker accent color to keep an all-white room from looking too bland. That's because when these two equal and opposite forces are in balance in our interior surroundings, we feel comfortable, secure, and at peace. Each aspect of our lives has yin and yang attributes that we need to balance.

When we explain these two forces in terms of the Feng Shui Elements, yin is represented by the color black, which is the Water Element, and the passive energy of silence, darkness, and slow, relaxed movements. This is the predominant energy at night when you go to sleep, or when you need to relax and replenish your energies, so it is often appropriate for bedrooms.

On the other hand, yang is represented by the color white, which is the Metal Element. It is the strong energy characterized by vibrant sounds and colors, bright lights, and upward moving energy. In Feng Shui, we would use yang energy in decorating a family room or a busy office.

Table 7.1 *Typical yin/yang balances in a home or office*

Yin	Yang
female	male
moonlight	darkness
quiet	noisy
even numbers	odd numbers
winter	summer
descending	ascending
cold	hot
curved	straight
empty	crowded
dark	light
bad smells	good smells
quiet	noisy
small	large
soft	hard
floral	geometric
smooth	textured
empty	abundant
open space	filled space

Table 7.1 displays some of the more familiar yin/yang balances you might find in a typical home or office.

Yin-Yang Balance in Commercial Spaces

Yin-yang theory is especially apparent in restaurants and retail stores. For example, think about dining in a restaurant that I will call the "Red Tomato Café." This dining space has red walls, high intensity lighting, loud music, hard metal chairs, abstract art on the walls, and tables arranged in long lines. The strong yang energy in this space stimulates you, makes you eat quickly, talk loudly, and feel excited. The management has created a restaurant that has quick turnover so they can be sure to fill the tables several times during the dinner hours. My guess is that you would naturally avoid the Red Tomato Café if you had a rough day at the office because you can't relax with all the activity around you.

Now, consider the restaurant I named "Mediterranean Breezes." In this space, the chairs are covered with fabric, there are earthy colors on the walls, plush carpet on the floors, soft music, low lighting, and round tables with tablecloths and candles, staggered randomly around the room. This restaurant is the type of space you would choose to celebrate an anniversary or relax with a glass of wine after a hard day. The softer yin energy of this space makes you feel relaxed. Management doesn't expect to turn tables as quickly in a space with yin energy and plans for patrons to linger and order more food and drink.

The same power of yin and yang is present in retail stores. First, think about the energy inside your neighborhood quick mart. This kind of space is characterized by harsh lighting, metal fixtures, and crowded shelves, all of which combine to make a yang environment. But since all you want is to pick up one item and get out of there, this quick energy is appropriate. In contrast, think of an upscale department store, where the softer lighting, round racks of clothing, upholstered chairs where spouses can wait comfortably, and light background music make you linger and look through the collections long enough until you finally buy something — often more than you planned to buy.

The yin-yang balance is especially important in the workplace where all too often we find ourselves working in less than optimal Feng Shui conditions. The typical office today is filled with computers, bright florescent lighting, hard shiny floors, metal filing cabinets and desks, and ringing phones that can result in strain, tension, irritability, and feelings of isolation. It is hard to feel creative in this kind of workplace because there is too much harsh yang energy. A little bit of yin energy balance, in the form of soft fabrics, desk and floor lamps instead of overhead lighting, wood filing cabinets, and some soothing colors on the walls would go a long way to balance this space.

Adjusting Yin and Yang

If the energy in your home or office just doesn't feel right, chances are good it is caused by a problem with the yin-yang balance. Fortunately, there are simple ways to add the attributes of yin and yang and restore balance.

Does your space need more *yin*? If you want to create a space that is more relaxed and focused, add:

- curves and flowing shapes
- dark colors

- upholstered furniture
- hanging light fixtures and lighting on dimmers
- shades on the windows
- rugs on the floors
- rooms with lots of furniture

Does your space need more *yang*? If you want to create a space full of energy and excitement, add:

- straight lines and angular shapes
- light and bright colors
- furniture made from wood, glass, or stone
- track lighting and bright lights
- wood blinds
- floors made from wood, marble, tile
- rooms with few pieces of furniture

CHAPTER
8

POWER PRINCIPLE #5:
CONTINUITY &
CONNECTEDNESS

It's not what you look at that matters; it's what you see.
~Henry David Thoreau

his power principle is related to the concept of the Tao (pronounced *dow*) in classical Feng Shui. Tao means "the way" or "the path," and contemporary approaches to Feng Shui define Tao as continuity or connectedness.

Because every action has a reaction, we are influenced by everything around us and, in turn, we influence everything. Related to this is my Feng Shui mantra: *you are what you see.* That is, the colors, shapes, and images you use to decorate your surroundings will influence what you attract into your life. The more you surround yourself with symbols of what you want to attract into your life — especially wealth, harmony, and love — the more likely you are to achieve it.

For example, if you surround yourself with artwork that is bleak and expresses isolation, you will attract the kinds of things and experiences that make you feel isolated and lonely. If you hold on to furniture that is shabby and worn, your life will feel impoverished. If you allow your faucets to drip and your toilets to run, your wealth will drain away.

However, if your artwork consists of images that express prosperity and joy, your life will be prosperous and joyous. If your furniture is up to date, clean, and comfortable, you will feel abundant. If your plumbing works, you will feel like your wealth is not drying up.

These contrasts show the difference between what I call a *prosperity consciousness* and a *poverty mentality*. That is, the more you surround yourself with symbols of what you want to attract into your life — especially wealth, harmony, and love — the more of those goals you will achieve.

The poet Maya Angelou said that we must be careful about the words we speak because the words will hang on the walls. While Angelou was writing about what we do in the figurative sense, Feng Shui believes that it is true of what we hang on our walls in the literal sense. That is why it is so important to surround yourself with uplifting images throughout your home.

Artwork that is depressing or shows images that are violent or unhappy will make you feel the same way. But artwork that is inspiring and reflects harmony and happiness will make you upbeat and receptive to good things coming into your life.

You can reinforce connectedness by adding symbols of the natural world to your interior environment, such as flowers, plants, rocks, water, nature sounds, artwork of nature scenes, and aromas, textures, and colors. When you bring the natural world inside, you bring peace and harmony to your life. The easiest way to bring the natural world inside is by selecting uplifting artwork that shows beautiful scenery. As an added benefit, when you bring the natural world inside, you bring in peace, harmony, and calmness to your life.

Landscapes are especially useful in activating positive energy; just be sure to avoid any images of swamps, dead trees, or decaying cities since they represent stagnant energy. Similarly, despite the fact that water represents flow and movement in Feng Shui, an image of the raging ocean could make you feel unsettled.

To see how your current artwork might be affecting your life, walk through your home and take a look at what is hanging on your walls from the perspective of your new Feng Shui "eyes." Consider whether each piece reflects what you want to attract into your life. If any piece is sending the wrong message, it's time to replace it, no matter how valuable it is.

The following are some ideas for choosing the right artwork to achieve various goals:

- If you want to power-up your career and attract more wealth, place water images in your Career/Work area.

- If you want to enhance friendships, hang images of happy people and joyous occasions in your Family/Community area.

- If you want to travel, hang international scenes or pictures of maps and globes in your Helpful People/Compassion area.

- If you want to attract or enhance love, hang images with pairs of objects like birds that mate for life or loving couples in your Love/Romance area.

You Are What You See

Everyone can use Feng Shui to feel connected to the natural world, but you don't have to decorate your home like a Chinese restaurant or a Zen shrine to bring the power of Feng Shui into your life. Although many Feng Shui symbols and objects are sold on Feng Shui websites or in New Age stores, they are not necessarily helpful in practicing contemporary Feng Shui. In the more Asian approaches to Feng Shui, displaying objects like a lucky money frog or a gold sailing ship are supposed to bring quick money or the perfect love. While there certainly can be a preferred place to keep these objects, they are not going to have a significant effect on your life unless they have specific meaning for you.

All of those so-called Feng Shui enhancements — including fu dogs, dragons, laughing Buddhas, red envelopes, bamboo fluids, and red streamers — are part of Chinese culture but not necessarily part of Feng Shui. If these objects don't symbolize anything to you and don't fit with your décor, they won't help you attract what you want into your life.

Buying a Feng Shui object with the hope that it will take care of all of your problems has been called the "vending machine approach" to Feng Shui — the belief that some selected object will automatically give you what you want. Unless you bring your own symbolic value to an object, it will not affect your life, no matter where you place it.

Instead, surround yourself with items that relate to specific goals you want to achieve, or objects or colors you love, so you can shift the energy of your home or office in a way that matches your own style. For example, personal symbols or icons related to your goals or personality traits — such as eagles, butterflies, or hearts — can be powerful Feng Shui enhancers. My personal icons are Dorothy's ruby red shoes and the phrase "there's no place like home," because they are a powerful reminder of how I help my clients achieve harmony with their homes.

The images you choose should represent a positive, clear idea of what you want to bring into each aspect of your life, since using objects or colors you love will attract what you love into your life. A so-called *traditional* Feng Shui object that you don't find attractive will not fix anything for you.

You are what you see. The most effective way to make adjustments is to choose objects that are symbols of your hopes and dreams in a particular area of your life. For example, if you want to enhance your relationship with your spouse, instead of buying a pair of Feng Shui fu dogs for your bedroom, hang a romantic picture of a place you have visited together, or a scene with a couple holding hands.

Feng Shui adjustments work best when the objects you choose to place in your home or office become visual reminders of what you want to attract into your life. Choose objects and colors that you love, so you can shift the energy of your home or office in a way that feels like you. It will be far more effective if you select everyday objects that you like and that match your home décor, in the shapes and colors that correspond to the bagua areas, instead of purchasing an object just because it has the words *Feng Shui* attached to it.

SUCCESS STORY:

Kevin's Sailing Ship

When I arrived for a home consultation with Kevin, he complained that his gold sailing ship wasn't working. The eighteen-inch ship was on a table in his living room. He told me he had read on a Feng Shui website that displaying the ship would make wealth sail into his home. But Kevin admitted that he didn't even like the ship, and he was spending money as fast as he earned it. I explained that if any object he displayed meant nothing to him, it wouldn't have any effect on his life. Only by surrounding himself with objects and images that represented his personal goals would he succeed in achieving them. To make matters worse, Kevin had placed his ship so it pointed out of the room instead of into the room, a symbol of wealth sailing right out of his life. Kevin quickly sold the ship on eBay, then used the proceeds to buy a print of a villa in Tuscany, a place he and his wife hoped to visit. Soon their cash flow started to improve, and they were able to save for their trip.

The most effective way to make adjustments is to choose an object as a symbol based on how it inspires, encourages, or empowers you in that area of your life, rather than for what they are supposed to do for you. Then, put these objects in your home in the appropriate bagua areas as a visual reminder of the positive steps you are taking toward making improvements in that area of your life.

Eight Tools of Feng Shui

There are many tools and objects you can use to cure, or fix, negative situations in your home or office and increase your feelings of continuity and connectedness. The eight categories of Feng Shui tools listed in table 8.1 on the following page are especially helpful to balance complementary forces and achieve harmony in your home or office.

With a knowledge of the five power concepts — *Chi, The Five Elements, The Bagua, Yin and Yang, Continuity and Connectedness* — you are almost ready to make improvements in your life.

But before you can use them effectively, you first need to clear your clutter.

Table 8.1 *Eight categories of Feng Shui tools for balancing complementary forces*

Tool	Uses
Color	Color adds context to our lives. We are conditioned to associate certain things with color, such as holidays, cultural events, and emotions. In Feng Shui, color is also used to represent and balance the Elements.
Sound	Sound, specifically music, is a powerful way to uplift the chi in any environment and to soothe stress in the home or office. Other sound makers such as wind chimes attract, or *call*, the chi into your home or workplace.
Lighting	Lighting, especially full-spectrum light bulbs that simulate natural light, is a simple way to bring more chi into your environment. Fireplaces and candles are also a source of light. Outside, garden lighting can be used to anchor a missing bagua area.
Artwork	Art of any kind, whether it is a painting, sculpture, or textiles, can enhance the chi. The selection of art should reflect positive images and feelings. The placement of your art depends on the area of the bagua you want to enhance.
Living Things	Plants, flowers, and animals add active chi. Use silk if your light is too limited to grow healthy plants or when you have allergies, but avoid dried flowers because they represent stagnant, dead energy. Keep animal cages and sleeping areas clean.
Water	Water features such as fountains, fish tanks, and waterfalls stimulate the movement of chi in and around your home or workplace. It is important to choose a sound of moving water that is appealing rather than disturbing.
Wind Sensitive Objects	Outside of your home, wind chimes, and other movement-sensitive objects such as mobiles, whirligigs, banners, and flags can be used to attract or *call* the chi toward your home to direct its positive energy.
Mirrors	Inside, mirrors can be used to reflect a pleasant view into a home or to symbolically move a wall and correct its shape; outside, they can be used to deflect a negative structure or unpleasant object.

PART THREE

The Feng Shui Clutter Clinic

A house is a place to keep your stuff, while you go get more stuff, until you have so much stuff, you have to go get a bigger house.
~ George Carlin

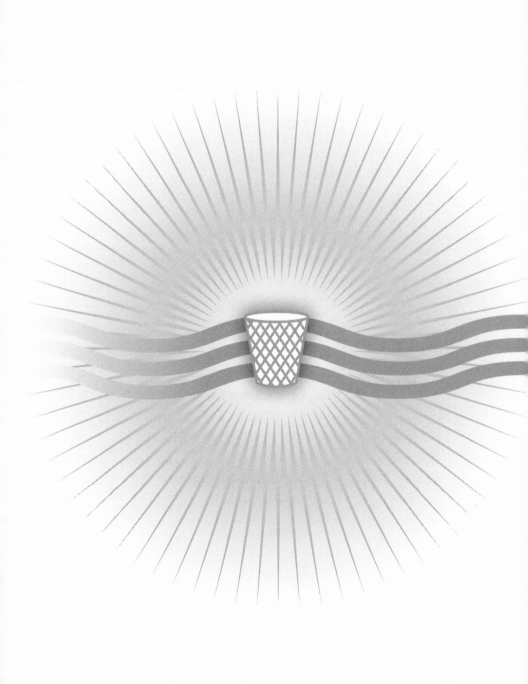

CHAPTER 9

JUST SAY THROW

You can't have everything. Where would you put it?
~ Steven Wright

*T*here is a story making the rounds among Feng Shui consultants about the wise Feng Shui practitioner and the confused, cluttered client.

When the wise practitioner walked into the cluttered client's home, all she could see were piles of paper everywhere.

"There are two types of people," the wise practitioner said to the client, "those who put their papers in files, and those who put their papers into piles."

"Which is better," the cluttered client asked, "the one who files or the one who piles?"

"The one who throws things away," said the wise practitioner.

In Feng Shui, clutter represents postponed decisions and the inability to move forward. What do you accumulate, where do you put it, and why do you keep it? The answers say a lot about you.

We all have to deal with some amount of clutter, but in Feng Shui terms, extreme clutter holds you back and keeps you from making progress.

One of the basic tenets of Feng Shui is that *nothing new flows into your life until you make room for it*. Therefore, clearing clutter is the key to transforming your space. Feng Shui is about attracting abundance into your life, but clutter blocks abundance from reaching you.

Clutter in Feng Shui is defined as anything unfinished, unused, unresolved, or hopelessly disorganized. Clutter creates stagnation, encouraging a negative "putting-off-until-tomorrow" mentality rather than a positive "doing-it-today" focus, thereby reducing energy in our minds and in our spaces.

Since things that are loved and used have strong, active energy around them, when you surround yourself with your favorite things, you add clarity and focus to your life. By contrast, when you surround yourself with things that you no longer love, or that hold negative memories, or are no longer useful, your life can lack direction.

Clutter represents stagnant energy. It keeps you in the past, encourages procrastination, contributes to a lack of harmony in your home, and makes you feel tired, overwhelmed, confused, angry, stuck, and depressed.

Clutter is one of the biggest issues that many of my clients face. If you want to deal with clutter once and for all, I offer this Feng Shui challenge: clear the clutter from one drawer, one closet, or one room today, and watch what good things flow into your life to take the place of all that mess tomorrow.

Studies show that of all the things we keep, we will only reuse one item in twenty. That means that most people *pile* rather than *file*, cluttering their spaces with things they never use. Many people with clutter problems can't solve them because when they think of getting rid of things, they experience fear of loss. They are afraid that if they throw away items they have been saving they might never be able to replace them. One way to avoid having to face the fear of getting rid of your clutter is to avoid accumulating things in the first place. Try turning any fears around: when you receive something — like a gift you don't really like or a memo you don't really need to save — ask yourself "how can I get rid of this" rather than "where can I keep it."

Where You Have Clutter

According to Feng Shui principles, a home is the outer manifestation of what is going on inside of the person. If you are outwardly cluttered with piles of laundry in the bedroom, stacks of magazines in the family room, disorderly files all over your desk, there is most likely an equal amount of disorder going on inside your mind. Piles of clutter in your home and office allow energy to stagnate, resulting in fatigue, lethargy, and often depression.

Cluttered, overcrowded environments create negative chi and affect your ability to move forward. When you remove clutter, you open up the flow of positive chi into your home and workplace and consequently into your life. And you just feel better.

Table 9.1 *Clutter locations and what they may reveal*

Where You Have Clutter...	What It May Be Concealing...
Entrance of a home	*Fear of relationships*
Inside a closet	*Unwillingness to examine emotions*
In a kitchen	*Resentment of care-taking*
Next to a bed	*Desire for change or escape*
Under a bed	*Fear of relationships*
On a desk	*Frustration, fear of letting go, need to control*
Behind a door	*Detachment from others*
Under a piece of furniture	*Concern with appearances*
In a basement	*Procrastination*
In an attic	*Living in the past*
In a garage	*Inability to actualize self*
All over	*Anger and low self-esteem*

Where and *why* you have clutter says a lot about what is going on in your life. A cluttered space equals a cluttered mind. If you look at clutter all day, clutter is what you will attract into your life. Table 9.1 reveals some common clutter locations and what they might reveal about hidden aspects of your life.

Clutter at Home

There is no good place to store your clutter, since in Feng Shui each part of your home represents one of nine bagua attributes you want to attract into your life — wealth, reputation, love, creativity, helpful people, career, harmony, health, grounding. Clutter in any one of the nine areas has a negative effect on the corresponding attribute. For example, clutter in Lisa's wealth area was affecting her cash flow.

SUCCESS STORY:
Lisa's Cash Flow

Lisa called me to arrange a home consultation because she never seemed to have enough money and was intrigued by the possibility that Feng Shui could help solve her problem. Lisa's living room was in the Wealth area of her home, but it was overflowing with unruly collections of old magazines, books, unwatched Netflix, and several weeks' worth of laundry to fold. I explained how this clutter was symbolically burying her wealth. I recommended she make it a priority to clear out the clutter and buy some good cabinets to hold the things she was keeping. After removing the clutter from the room, Lisa found that her cash was flowing again and she could balance her checkbook each month.

A good Feng Shui clutter-clearing can help you determine what items to keep and why, especially when it comes to what you accumulate in your closets. Unlike wine, clothes rarely improve with age. So if you haven't worn something in a year, if it doesn't fit right, or you don't feel good when you wear it, it's time to toss it or donate it to a local charity where it can do some good.

This includes old clothes you may be keeping in the hopes of losing twenty-five pounds you have not been able to lose for years. If you plan to lose that much weight to wear an item of clothing, it is highly unlikely you will want to wear your old, out-of-style stuff when you do succeed at weight loss. You will want — and deserve — brand new clothes! So move out those old clothes today, and make room for new clothes, in smaller sizes, to fill your closet.

Clutter at the Office

Picture yourself in your office surrounded by a sea of paperwork, trying to find that memo about the meeting you are about to attend and muttering the phrase, "It's here, somewhere!" If you don't have to think too hard to put yourself in this picture, it's time to do something about workplace clutter.

Clutter in an office or workspace slows productivity (because of wasted time spent looking for misplaced things), increases stress, and prevents new ideas and business opportunities from manifesting. Studies show that people spend an average of 30 percent of their work time hunting for documents buried under phone messages, sticky notes, paper piles, or personal items, such as coffee mugs, cell phones, and framed photos. And that doesn't even include clutter on your computer screen and in your hard drive.

One study by *Fast Company Magazine* found that executives waste six weeks per year searching for lost documents — time, which if better spent, might even result in a promotion. Think of what you could accomplish if you gave yourself an extra six weeks back.

If you want to have new ideas, attract clients, or make progress in your business, get rid of desktop clutter, clean out file cabinets, and clear your hard drive and you will make room for new projects, customers, and ideas.

The following example shows how clutter in a workspace affected a small business.

SUCCESS STORY:
Ed's Growing Business

When he contacted me for a Feng Shui consultation, Ed's home repair business was suffering; sales were down and his morale was low. I immediately noticed his small, cluttered desk, his mismatched collection of cast-off furniture, and his dented filing cabinets. And there was paper everywhere. I suggested Ed buy a larger desk to symbolize more room for his business to grow, clear out and consolidate his files so he needed less storage space, and get rid of all the excess paper that was distracting him from his business goals. He immediately ordered new furniture, bought a shredder, and shredded all unnecessary documents. Within a few weeks of his clutter reduction project, Ed's customer base dramatically improved, sales began increasing, and his confidence in his ability to succeed was restored.

Feng Shui Forward

Clutter often reflects living in the past, and getting rid of it paves the way for you to move forward. If you let go of clutter, you let go of the reason for holding on to objects that are not supporting you and open up your life to new possibilities. This doesn't mean you have to discard all of your treasured objects and memories. It just means that you have to take a hard look at what you are defining as "treasure," keeping only mementos that are really important to you and inspire you, and getting rid of other items that are simply holding you in the past without any positive value.

The following story shows how you can hold on to mementos from an old relationship without even realizing they are affecting you in a negative way.

SUCCESS STORY:

Brenda's New Romance

Brenda wanted a new relationship in her life. I recommended she start making changes in her front hall closet and clearing out the clutter that represented her ex-husband. I explained to Brenda that her entry is where positive energy first enters her home, and that removing clutter from an entry closet is a great way to make room for a new love to walk through her front door. Brenda began tossing items reflecting memories of her former marriage, including a box of yellowed wedding photos and her ex's old athletic shoes and baseball caps she had forgotten about — all clutter that represented what had been wrong in the relationship. Within a month, Brenda met a wonderful man at a friend's house, and she is well on her way to starting over with a new relationship.

Psychologists have identified numerous reasons and mental blocks that influence why we hold on to things and create clutter. The good news is that a few simple Feng Shui quick fixes, as shown in table 9.2, can start you on the road to overcoming these blocks.

The 5-Step Clutter-Clearing Process

Where do I start? It's a frequent question I hear from clients who need to do some serious clutter clearing. Most people get overwhelmed when it is time to clear out the garage, the basement, that closet, or even one *junk* drawer. They set aside an entire weekend to get it done, but when the time finally arrives, so do the excuses: the weather is too beautiful, the sky is too gray, they're feeling too tired. Most people find it too overwhelming to attack all of that clutter at once, so consequently nothing gets done.

To help overcome this inertia, I developed the following simple *5-Step Feng Shui Clutter-Clearing Process* to help bust clutter without getting overwhelmed. The trick is to pick a time and a place, then do a little every day until you conquer your clutter hot spots. Fortunately, each day of clutter clearing will help give you the self-confidence, satisfaction, and momentum to continue.

Table 9.2 *Feng Shui quick fixes for overcoming clutter*

Symptoms	Issue	Feng Shui Quick Fix
• Buying in bulk • Cooking in large quantities • Guilt over wasting things • Inability to throw away	**Need for Abundance**	Designate a place for everything and keep everything in its place!
• Keeping objects from deceased relatives too long • Holding on to objects that no longer serve a purpose	**Holding on to the Past**	Choose a few small keepsakes from people you loved and dispose of the rest!
• Keeping unfinished projects • Inability to be satisfied with your work	**Perfectionism**	Finish one half-finished project and throw out the rest!
• Collecting things you do not need • Bouncing from task to task	**Inability to Set Priorities**	Create a system that works for you and stick to it!
• Creating excuses for not moving forward • Hiding behind your disorganization	**Fear of Failure/ Fear of Success**	Start with baby steps and slowly move forward on one small project!
• Holding on to things "just in case" you need them • Fearing that you won't be able to afford to replace something you discard	**Poverty Mentality**	Approach the world from prosperity consciousness — the belief that you will always have what you need!

The following are six general guidelines to keep in mind when using the *5-Step Feng Shui Clutter-Clearing Process*:

1. Clear clutter with a *prosperity consciousness* (that is, reassure yourself that you can afford to replace the item in the

future if you need it) rather than a *poverty mentality* (the idea that you might never have enough money to replace the object in the future).

2. Avoid clutter clearing when you are sad, depressed, or angry; wait until you are feeling more like yourself. You may make bad decisions when you are sad, depressed, or angry and thus clear clutter for the wrong reasons or eliminate the wrong items.

3. If you are undecided about getting rid of an object, ask yourself: What is the worst thing that can happen to me if I let go of this object? Unless you would suffer extreme negative consequences, let the object go.

4. Instead of holding on to all of your family mementos, keep small, representative keepsakes of special family holidays and special moments, such as a swatch of fabric from a party or prom dress, and let go of the rest.

5. If you receive a gift or inheritance from someone you love but you do not love the gift, donate it to your favorite charity, or pass it on to someone who will appreciate it more.

6. If you have accumulated items that you are going to sell, donate, or throw out *some day in the future...* that day is here! Start today and avoid any more procrastination.

Day One

Step 1

Start clutter clearing by setting aside 20 to 30 minutes. Put on your favorite piece of music and begin anywhere in your home or office.

Step 2

Pick up an item and decide if you are keeping it. If you are keeping it, place it in its permanent home.

Step 3

If you are removing an object, place it into one of four piles:

- *Trash* (hopefully, the largest pile)
- *Donate* (items that are still usable)
- *Sell* (objects for sale, consignment, online auctions)
- *Decide* (things you cannot decide whether to toss or keep)

Step 4

While the music plays, keep sorting and placing your things. When the music stops, you are done for the day. Pat yourself on the back for a job well done.

Step 5

Dispose of your piles in this way:

- *Trash*: Immediately take these items out to the garbage.

- *Donate*: Call your favorite charity and make an appointment for a pickup.

- *Sell*: Go online and list your stuff on websites like *www.ebay.com*, *www.craigslist.com*, *www.freecycle.com*, or similar service; place an ad in the local newspaper; set a date on your calendar to take a load of stuff to a consignment shop.

- *Decide*: Put these items in a black plastic bag and place them in the trunk of your car. Drive around with them for 30 days, and if you do not need them during that time — *drive directly to the nearest charity drop box and get rid of the bag!*

Day Two and Beyond

Repeat Steps 1 through 5 each day, preferably at the same time of day but not necessarily in the same place. Do this for 30 days and you will rapidly work through even your most cluttered spaces. You can move from room to room each day, or continue in the same room. Then you can sit back and enjoy the positive results that fill the open spaces you have created. ▲▬❖❙

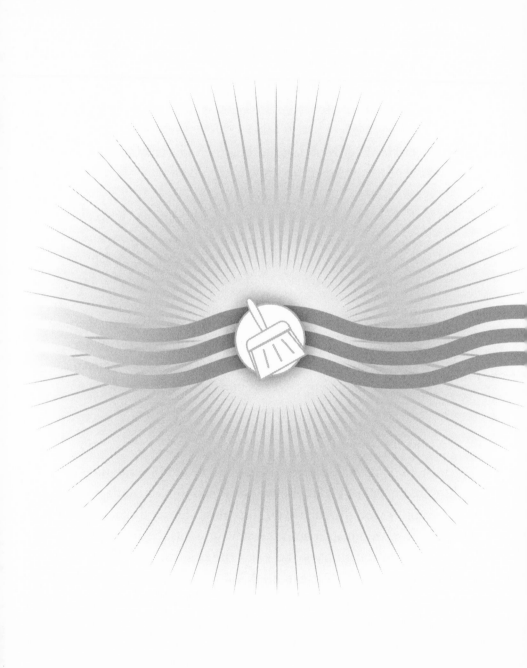

CHAPTER
10

MONTH-BY-MONTH CLUTTER CLEARING

There comes a time when you have to let your clothes
go out into the world and try to make it on their own.
~ Bette Midler

Now that you have a basic understanding of how clutter affects your life and how you can gain control over it by using the *5-Step Feng Shui Clutter-Clearing Process*, you are ready to embark on my month-by-month clutter-clearing program. Here are twelve months' worth of my favorite Feng Shui clutter-clearing tips that clients have used with great success. The tips are organized seasonally, but you can start with the current month and work through a complete year.

JANUARY: Take a Feng Shui Fling

Start your year out right by doing the Feng Shui fling. On trash day, take a large plastic trash bag, move quickly through your home, and fling 27 things into the bag — things you don't need, don't want, or don't know why you are keeping. Open drawers and cabinets. Dig down under the sink. Don't analyze, don't hesitate, just fling. Then take the bag right out to your trashcan before you change your mind. (Three is an especially auspicious number in Feng Shui, and because the number 27 includes multiple sets of three, your flinging will be especially prosperous.) Do the Feng Shui fling once a week this month, then stand back to watch good things flow into the open spaces you have created.

FEBRUARY: Make Room for a Relationship

In this month of Valentine's Day, remove clutter from your house to open up space for the perfect partner to come into your life. Even if you are already in a loving relationship, clearing clutter will strengthen it. Your goal is to free up 25 percent of the space in your home, especially your bedroom, for someone else's things. Start with these critical places:

- Clear out your bedroom closet, so there will be room for your lover's clothes, and add some extra hangers.

- Throw away old food like leftovers from the refrigerator and packages of stale crackers and broken chips from the pantry to leave space for another person's favorite foods.

- Toss expired prescriptions and used-up toothpaste tubes

to make an opening in the medicine cabinet or bathroom vanity for a lover's toiletries.

- Clear off one of the night tables in the bedroom and empty at least one drawer so there will be an open space for a new partner's items.

- Clear your bed of extra decorative pillows, throws, and stuffed animals so there will be room for a lover to join you in bed.

MARCH: Let Your Old Clothes Go

As the weather starts to change, transform your wardrobe by letting go of the clothes you no longer need, such as shoes that cause blisters, pants that ride a bit too high in the crotch, skirts and suits from your button-down days, or the clothes that are sizes too small. Even though you may have paid a lot for them and loved them when you bought them, if you haven't worn an item of clothing for a year, remove it from your closet and donate it to charity. When you hold on to things that don't fit, you hold on to old energy and symbolically hold on to excess weight. Whether you donate them, sell them, or just put them out with the trash, getting rid of unworn clothing makes room for a bounty of new clothes — often in a smaller size — to come your way.

APRIL: Ask Three Taxing Questions

Congratulate yourself on making it through another tax season, which can promote clutter due to record keeping and tax filing. Tax professionals recommend keeping personal tax records for five to seven years, but you can safely shred at least one box of your oldest tax records each year after you file your tax return. To determine what to keep in addition to what is required by law, answer these three questions for an easy way to decide whether a piece of paper is clutter or a keeper:

1. *If I throw this away, will I get arrested?* If the answer is no, toss it!

2. *Did I need this during the last year?* If the answer is no, toss it!

3. *Can I get it someplace else, especially on the Internet?* If the answer is yes, toss it!

MAY: Clear Out the Kitchen

A clean, food-filled kitchen is a symbol of health and prosperity in Feng Shui. Here are some ways to clear kitchen clutter and encourage wealth to flow into your life:

- Throw out anything in your refrigerator and freezer that is old, half-full, or fuzzy.

- Update any old photos, take-out menus, or shopping lists

on the fridge door with new ones; remove tacky refrigerator magnets.

- Remove everything from your pantry, wipe the shelves, and get rid of any opened items more than six months old.

- Buy a new pair of oven mitts or potholders to replace the burnt ones.

- Refill canisters with fresh flour, sugar, rice, coffee, and tea bags.

- Thoroughly sweep the kitchen floor — toward the door — to symbolically sweep out the old negative energy and make room for good things.

JUNE: Spring Clean Your Office

When warmer weather puts you in the mood for some spring-cleaning, focus on your office:

- Clean your computer, including keyboard and monitor.

- Vacuum, sweep, or mop your floor; even if you have a cleaning service, doing it yourself helps to symbolically sweep out the old energy.

- Bundle up your electrical cords and wires and contain them with a twist tie or tubes made specially to control cords.

- Remove everything from your shelves and dust; put back only the books that you currently use and recycle the rest.

- Trim growth and remove the dead leaves from office plants; if you have silk plants, dust them, or replace them if they are faded.

- Wash your windows so your vision will be clear.

JULY: Read and Release

To avoid cramming books into an already crowded bookcase, practice the "read and release" principle. After you have read a book, give it to a friend, donate it to charity, *forget it* at Starbuck's, leave it at the grocery store, drop it on a park bench, or trade it at a used bookstore (with security concerns, it is probably best to avoid leaving books in airports and on planes.) Releasing your books makes room in your home for new things to flow into your life, while simultaneously enriching the universe by sharing the pleasure of reading with others.

AUGUST: Give Your Desk Drawer a Vacation

Before you leave for your summer vacation, give your desk a vacation from clutter. To quickly bust the clutter that had accumulated in your desk drawer, toss the following items into the trash:

- Dried-up pens and markers
- Bent and twisted paper clips

- Plastic knives, forks, ketchup, and mustard packets from take-out lunches
- Month-old memos
- Phone message slips from people you have already called
- Pencils with worn-down erasers
- Dried up bottles or tubes of correction fluid
- Brittle, cracked rubber bands
- Last year's planner
- Flyers for past events

SEPTEMBER: Organize School Papers

Although you may love all the drawings and papers that your children bring home from school, if you save them all the value of special ones is diminished since they get lost in the clutter. Instead, each week collect all of the papers in a folder and have your children select only several to keep. Put them on the refrigerator or display them on a bulletin board. After a week, date each paper and put them in a scrapbook or keepsake box for each child. If your children are grown and out of the house but you still have all of their papers, create scrapbooks of the best of their work. Give the rest of the accumulated papers back to your children to sort, throw away, or make their own scrapbooks.

OCTOBER: Control Mailbox Clutter

This is the month when the deluge of holiday catalogues starts arriving in your mailbox. And even if you pay bills online and register at anti-junk-mail websites, you probably still get too much printed mail. When all of that mail accumulates it translates into clutter. Since Feng Shui is all about movement, here are a few tips for moving your mail rather than accumulating it:

- Set up a mail sorting area near the recycling bin and shredder; when you bring in the mail, toss the junk into the bin and feed your shredder with any documents that have your social security or account numbers.

- Create in-baskets for everyone in the family, so when mail enters the house you can route it to the other appropriate family members.

- Set up e-billing and e-payment online so you will receive fewer items in the mail.

- Register at anti-junk-mail websites.

NOVEMBER: Give Thanks for Extra Space

In this month of Thanksgiving, you don't need more things to be thankful for; you just need more room for thankfulness. Here are five things you can get rid of this month and be thankful for the extra space in your life:

- One unfinished project
- One object that needs fixing but is not worth the effort

- One gift you never liked even though you love the gift giver
- One souvenir that no longer has meaning
- One item of clothing you have outgrown, physically or emotionally

DECEMBER: Reduce Guilt Clutter

End your year by reducing your guilt clutter: the guilt over getting rid of gifts that came from someone special, objects that cost you a lot of money, or items you bought but don't like or need. Your guilt-inducing items might include such things as the wool scarf from mom that you can't wear now that you moved to Florida; the electric fondue pot that your best friend gave you as a housewarming gift but is still in the box; the poster from the gallery opening you went to with your ex-boyfriend; the 144-piece tool set from dad for the workshop you never set up because you live in an apartment; the home gym equipment that is now a clothes rack. Stop feeling guilty and find a new home for all of these things: donate them, sell them online, or toss them today, and make space for new energy to flow into your life tomorrow.

The Fable of the Magic Red Geranium

Have you heard the fable of the *Magic Red Geranium*? A woman living in a shabby, cluttered house was given an enchanted red geranium by a wise person who told her to take it home, where it would transform her life. She took the geranium home and set it on her wobbly kitchen table covered by a stained tablecloth. Immediately, she saw how the beautiful form and color of the geranium made the wobbly table seem in disrepair and the table linen look shabby. So, she fixed the table leg and washed the tablecloth.

Then she noticed how her newly washed tablecloth made her floor seem dull, so she scrubbed it. This made her kitchen walls look drab, so she repainted the room in a fresh color and replaced missing cabinets knobs.

Eventually her entire home was sparkling, and she had indeed transformed her life.

Is there a room in your home that would benefit from a symbolic *red geranium* clutter clearing? Clearing out a drawer, a closet, or the garage can be like bringing a red geranium into your home to raise your awareness of other areas that need to be cleared of clutter. And the more clutter you clear, the more new energy and positive possibilities will open up to transform both your environment and your life.

Feng Shui is all about attracting abundance into your life. Clutter blocks that abundance from reaching you. Clutter in Feng Shui is defined as anything unfinished, unused, unresolved, just tolerated, and hopelessly disorganized. It includes those items in our surroundings that have no real home of their own. Clutter creates stagnation and therefore diminishes the energy in our spaces and in our minds. It encourages a sense of procrastination and a negative *putting-off-for-tomorrow* mentality rather than a positive *doing-it-today* abundance.

Things that are loved, used, and appreciated have strong, active energy around them. When you surround yourself with things you love, you add clarity and focus to your life. When you are surrounded by things that hold negative memories, things that are no longer useful, and things you do not love, your life can lack direction.

Choose one place to start clearing clutter, then step back and reap the reward of good things flowing into your life.

PART FOUR

Feng Shui Tips for All Seasons

Simplicity, simplicity, simplicity! I say, let your affairs
be as two or three, and not a hundred or a thousand,
instead of a million count half a dozen...
~ Henry David Thoreau

A YEAR OF TRANSFORMATIONS

People usually are the happiest at home.
~ William Shakespeare

Now that you have learned the basic Five Power Principles of Feng Shui and have started to clear some of your clutter, it is time to put what you have learned into everyday practice through the seasons of your life. I recommend you embark upon a year of Feng Shui transformations for your own home and office.

The practical magic of Feng Shui is different for every one of us, and when you embark upon your year of Feng Shui changes, the speed at which your transformations occur will be different as well. Sometimes a shift happens literally overnight, while other times if your behavior patterns are deeply ingrained, it can take weeks or even months for the effects of your Feng Shui improvements to appear.

That's what happened to Allison.

Allison felt stuck between "a rock and a hard place" when she contacted me to set up her Feng Shui home consultation. A relatively new real estate agent, her finances were strained because of a lingering downturn in the market. She had sold only a few of her listings since the beginning of the year and had not received a commission in months. To make matters worse, her roommate had moved out to live with a boyfriend and Allison could not afford to pay the rent on the pricey loft by herself. She was happy for her roommate, but was hoping that she, too, could find love.

To complicate the situation even more, Allison's aging car was no longer appropriate for chauffeuring her clients around to see houses, and she needed a new one. Allison was afraid her limited finances would make her choose between getting a new apartment and buying a new car.

To get her career and her life moving forward, I outlined a year of Feng Shui changes for Allison, starting with a thorough clutter clearing of her home to get rid of any negative energy and to remove the "single-girl" stuffed animals from her bedroom, followed by *powering-up* her office with images of high-end homes and properties to symbolically attract more listings and sales. Here is what Allison wrote about her year of Feng Shui changes:

SUCCESS STORY
Allison's Rock and Hard Place

Since I put Feng Shui to work for me last year, I have

paid in full for a new car, moved into a new fabulous apartment, and have fallen madly in love with a guy I met in the fitness center of my new complex. And to think that when I began this process, I thought I would have to choose between a car and an apartment! I felt so stuck when I first started making daily Feng Shui changes, but with slow and steady implementation of a day-by-day plan, I was able to gradually make things happen that I previously thought were impossible.

As Allison's success story illustrates, when the energy in a home or office has been *stuck* for a long time, or if your own behavior pattern is deeply ingrained, it can take a while until you see any obvious results. Be patient and watch for the small signs that things are moving, like the synchronicity of thinking about something and having it appear somehow on your personal radar screen.

Everyday Adjustments Throughout the Seasons

The goal of Feng Shui adjustments for your home or office is to bring your interior environment in balance with the natural world around you. The best way to do this is to make it an everyday habit to tune in to the changing seasons and make changes in your home and office to reflect what is going on around you at different times of the year.

Seasonal Practice

As you begin this everyday practice of Feng Shui, let your personality and tastes be your guide for choosing objects and colors to make your changes work for you. Even small, everyday Feng Shui adjustments practiced consistently through the seasons can yield big results.

For example, at the beginning of the year you can make changes that relate to clearing old energy out of your home and office, especially reducing the clutter around you. Since clutter keeps you from moving forward, removing it from your surroundings at this season will help you enter the year with a "clean slate."

Then, as you approach the winter days with their limited daylight, make adjustments that bring more light and color into your interior environment, such as switching to full spectrum light bulbs that simulate natural daylight, or remembering to buy fresh flowers at the beginning of each week. This is a good time to consider adding color to your workspace to energize your career; for example, red has stimulating qualities that are perfect for salespeople; blues and greens provide inspiration for people in IT careers; warm earthy colors encourage collaboration in all career fields.

When spring bursts on the scene you can begin to focus on changes that mirror the growth all around you. This could be as simple as buying new houseplants, or giving your old ones a spring cleaning by pruning dead leaves and adding a good dose of fertilizer. Another way to "green up" is to replace your current art with images that show growing things, like a beautiful meadow of spring tulips or daffodils. Since this is the mid-point in the year, make it the half-way point in your season of Feng Shui changes as well by conducting a "Feng Shui audit" to make sure the cures you have put in place are still working for you. Make any adjustments or changes necessary for your improvements to continue to work their practical magic for you throughout the rest of the year.

As you enter the summer months that are associated with hot, yang energy, your focus could be on cooling down your home and office. Some simple changes include using cool blue sheets and a lighter weight comforter on your bed, and turning off the overhead fluorescent lights in your office and letting the natural daylight light your workplace.

When autumn approaches and you find yourself spending more time indoors, you can begin some of those projects that you put off during the warmer months, like clearing all that *stuff* from your attic or basement. Clearing what you don't need from these areas can have a profound effect on your life because what is in your attic weighs down on you and what is in your basement supports your life in your home. Clutter in either of these areas keeps you from moving forward.

Keep in mind as you are making seasonal changes that Feng Shui cures will wear out over time and you do need to renew them occasionally: colors fade, furniture wears out or goes out of style, your preferences in art change. That's why I recommend that after you complete the year of Feng Shui tips in the next section in this book, you start again and *re-new*, *re-adjust,* and *re-align* your improvements.

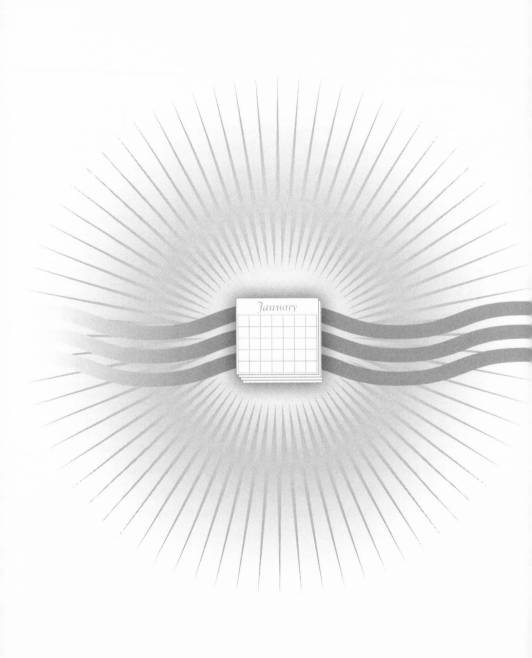

A CALENDAR OF 366 FENG SHUI TIPS

If there is harmony in the house,
there will be order in the nation.
~ Chinese Proverb

*T*o help you make seasonal changes in the coming year, I have pulled together a calendar of 366 tips, including one for leap year. This calendar is a compilation of my favorite Feng Shui advice to help you use the practical magic of Feng Shui, one day at a time, to deal with all of life's adventures and misadventures.

These tips pertain to people and pets; love, marriage, parenting, and divorce; remarriage and blended families; your home, your office, your car; all of the seasons, holidays, and celebrations of your life. I have included tips about your doors and windows, your kitchen and your dining room, your bedroom and your bathroom. There is advice about your clothes and your closets. The tips cover the adventures you have in summer, fall, winter, and spring. They

135

help strengthen your relationships with your spouse and your children, your friends and your family, and even provide some advice if your loved ones are deployed overseas.

Liberally sprinkled through this calendar of tips are success stories from my clients to illustrate how everyday people can make everyday Feng Shui changes to improve their lives.

The calendar on the following pages is presented one week at a time. Start now and work through the tips one-a-day. If you get to a tip that doesn't apply to your situation, use that day to work on a previous tip that you skipped. When you start using these tips, you will see an immediate improvement in specific aspects of your life. By the time you work through a full year of the Feng Shui tips and techniques, you will be amazed by the improvements in all aspects.

SUCCESS STORY:

Mary Anne's New Clients

I explained to Mary Anne that the most cluttered part of her kitchen was in her wealth area, and recommended she clear the clutter and display some images that represented prosperity. I told her that the fountain she had placed on the kitchen counter was symbolically putting out the "fire" in her wealth accumulation. When she sent me photos of the revitalized space, I could hardly believe it was the same room.

Mary Anne wrote:

I immediately worked on the wealth corner. I hung a new poster and cleaned out all extraneous stuff in the cabinet and on the counter, leaving only the most beautiful things. I have been intending for years that love and money come together for me. I had no place for a 1930s-style poster with a very queenly image until I realized the kitchen was the perfect location because it combined two goals for me. I had been running an ad in the local paper for more than a month with no response; last night, shortly after I moved the fountain to my office, I received two e-mails about my services. I signed two new clients the next day.

JANUARY

1	On New Year's Day **move 27 things** to encourage something new to happen in the coming year.
2	Clean out a **closet** today to make room for good things to flow into your life.
3	Buy **fresh flowers** to attract an abundance of auspicious energy into your home.
4	Give your home a **thorough cleaning** so you can begin the new year with a clean slate.
5	Remove the things stored **behind your doors** because doors that don't completely open represent blockage in your life.
6	**Open your front door** every day to encourage new energy, and consequently new wealth, to flow into your house.
7	Hang a mirror behind your stove or display a **shiny teakettle** to reflect the number of burners and symbolically double your wealth.

JANUARY

8 — Place a **fountain** or picture of flowing water in the foyer near the front door to attract the flow of positive energy into the house.

9 — To make your **reputation shine**, hang a picture of a sunrise or sunflowers in your office directly across from the door.

10 — Start a **new habit** today: keep the bathroom door closed to prevent positive chi from dumping into the toilet.

11 — Take the **trash** out through the back door or garage rather than the front door, where wealth enters your home.

12 — If the first thing you see when you walk into your home does not make you feel **happy to be home**, replace it with something upbeat.

13 — If you live in a house where the front and back doors are in a **direct line**, the chi runs straight out of your house; place a small rug in the foyer or hallway between the doors to slow the chi.

14 — To encourage positive energy to **enter your house** clean the front door and repaint or re-stain it, oil the hinges, and clean any windows.

JANUARY

15 If you have had an **argument** in your house recently, thoroughly clean it because negative chi can accumulate after harsh words are spoken in a house.

16 To invite wealth into your restaurant or **retail business**, keep the area around the cash register clear of clutter.

17 To strengthen your resolve to stick to a **diet** in the new year, place an object directly in the path into your kitchen; you will have to think about what you're doing before you get into the room.

18 Keep **pets** off of your bed, because when a pet sleeps between a couple, it represents splitting the relationship and deterring romance.

19 Buy a lush new plant and place it in the health area of your home or office to ensure a **healthy beginning** to the year.

20 If you want to **eat less** this year, slow down your eating by using blue plates since the color blue reduces appetite, as well as blood pressure and pulse rate.

21 Clear clutter from kitchen cabinets, drawers, counters, and the refrigerator to psychologically **lighten your kitchen** and, consequently, your weight.

JANUARY

22	To slow the chi moving down a **long hallway**, decorate it like a gallery or museum, hanging artwork of varying sizes at various heights.
23	Whether you call them **knickknacks**, tschotkes, or objet d'art, too many can block the flow of energy in a house; instead of displaying everything, rotate your favorites so you can see your entire collection throughout the year.
24	Throw away 27 things in your office to create an **opening for success** to flow into your career.
25	Take the **scenic route home** from work today to change your perspective, even if it takes longer; do this at least once a month.
26	Replace any **burned out** light bulbs in your house, preferably with high-efficiency bulbs, to recharge your own energy.
27	If you want to feel more **connected** to friends and family, hang artwork that has images of happy people and joyous events.
28	If you want to **find a new job**, decorate your workspace with objects that are green (Wood Element).

JANUARY

29	To **encourage abundance** in your life, decorate your living room with accents of red (Fire Element).
30	**Repair** broken and nonworking items in your workplace and you will fix what is not working in your career.
31	If you need to feel energized against the cold, **dark winter** day, wear blues and greens, plant-based fibers, floral patterns, and relaxed styles (Wood Element).

Matt's Expanding Business

The first time I did an office consultation for Matt, he was moving his software development business from his basement to leased space. I recommended he take the smaller of the two offices in the suite because it was in the power position, and give his marketing manager the office that occupied the relationship area. He reluctantly followed the advice, and six months later called to thank me and arrange another consultation. He was moving his growing company into bigger space and expanding from three staff members to seventeen. I recommended the most auspicious location for his office, and where to locate his managers. Eighteen months later, I was delighted to get more good news from Matt.

Matt wrote:

At our last consultation, you asked whether I believed that my Feng Shui changes had anything to do with the success of my company. My answer then was that it probably had and that was why I wanted another consultation. Well, my answer now is "of course" because we just landed our largest contract to date, and we are ready to sign a lease for half a floor in a new office building. I want you to take a look at the space before we move to make sure we locate everyone in the right place. Yes, this Feng Shui does work.

FEBRUARY

1	Place a **pair of objects**, such as candles, hearts, or vases, in your bedroom to enhance romance or marriage.
2	If your love life is going nowhere, get rid of pictures from a **past love**, since these tie you to the past and hold you back.
3	If you are a **single woman** looking for romance, hang several masculine-looking wood hangers in your closet to attract a lover's clothes.
4	If you are a **single male** looking for a mate, remove the posters of guy toys, like cars, bikes, or beer, from your bedroom.
5	Get rid of your bed from a previous relationship because when using it you are sleeping with your **former lover**.
6	For **Chinese New Year**, clean and remove clutter from your kitchen; a clean, food-filled kitchen is the center of family life and a symbol of health and prosperity for the new year.
7	To improve your love life, remove **photographs** of your children, parents, and pets from your bedroom so they won't be "watching" you in bed.

FEBRUARY

8	To encourage more **intimacy** in a relationship, display photos of you and your spouse or significant other doing something fun or romantic together.
9	If you are looking for romance, avoid hanging artwork that shows only a **single person** or a scene reflecting loneliness in your bedroom or the love area of your home.
10	If your **love life** has gone stale, buy new sheets and a comforter to freshen your relationship.
11	Buy yourself a **gift** today as a symbol to affirm that you will have continuing prosperity and be able to afford whatever you want.
12	Make sure you have the **right-sized bed** for your relationship; if the bed is too big, partners can drift apart; if it is too small, they can feel trapped in the relationship.
13	Plan a **romantic dinner** for two, ideally at a square or round table with no more than two extra chairs; too many chairs can make you feel like you are having a party and the guests didn't show.
14	If you give **roses** as a gift on Valentine's Day or any other occasion, remove the thorns to assure a smooth romance.

FEBRUARY

15	Place a pair of **night tables** in your bedroom to invite a partner into your bed and equality into your relationship.
16	To attract a new relationship into your life, clear out some space in your medicine cabinet to make room for a **lover's toiletries**.
17	To encourage harmony in your **marriage**, combine black and white in your decor to balance the yin-yang aspects of your lives together.
18	If you sleep in a **bedroom above a garage**, place a thick carpet on the floor to keep the negative energy from the void underneath you from affecting your health.
19	Make sure your bedroom is more yin (dark and quiet) than yang (bright and noisy) to assure a **blissful rest** and a loving relationship.
20	For a **harmonious relationship** between couples, display images or real bunches of peonies in the living room.
21	If you want to get **pregnant**, display images of mothers and children in the Relationship, Children, or Family areas of your house.

FEBRUARY

22	If you want to attract a romantic partner into your home, make room in the pantry and **refrigerator** for his or her favorite foods.
23	If you want to attract a new relationship, clear out space in the bedroom closet so there will be room for a **lover's clothes**.
24	If you want to add passion to your love life, sleep on pink **sheets**, which increase the yang energy that enhances feelings of love and romance.
25	If you want to **earn more money**, display art in your office that shows a waterfall or river, which are associated with a prosperous career and increasing income.
26	If you want to attract a new love into your life, get rid of old **love letters** because you need to let go of old love before new love can enter your heart.
27	If you want a new romance, remove the **extra pillows**, blankets, and stuffed animals from your bed because they send the message that you have no room for anyone else to join you.
28	To help romance blossom, hang a picture of a **pair of cranes**; they mate for life and therefore symbolize devotion and togetherness.
29	On **leap year** place a healthy plant in the wealth area of your home so your wealth will flourish throughout the year.

A Surprise in Helen's Closet

The American Dream may be a house with so much closet space that you and your spouse or partner can have separate closets, but according to Feng Shui it is preferable that a couple share a closet because their energies mingle, enhancing the relationship. This doesn't mean you have to give up an individual closet. I often recommend that couples with separate closets exchange some items of clothing to keep in each other's closet, such as a favorite sweater, a purse, or a shirt. Helen took this advice to a heart.

Helen wrote:

When my husband came home from a business trip, even though it was late at night he immediately found what I had hung in his closet...my lace and satin panties and a satin garter belt on a satin hanger. He got a real kick out of it! Now we are trying to decide what items of his to hang in my closet.

MARCH

1	To help your **career soar**, decorate your office with pictures of objects taking off, such as a flock of birds flying or hot air balloons rising.
2	Display plants with rounded leaves in you wealth area, especially **African violets** and jade plants, because this shape represents coins and therefore wealth.
3	If you have a favorite **burner** on your stove or cook top, try using a different one to cook dinner tonight; burners represent wealth and using only one limits your income.
4	Move your **computer** out of the bedroom, since the electromagnetic frequencies can keep you from sleeping; if you can't move it, turn it off at night.
5	Avoid sleeping with your **feet** pointed directly out the bedroom door, known as the "death position"; if you can't move the bed, use a footboard or put furniture at the foot for protection.
6	If your **bathroom** is across from the front door, keep the door closed and hang colorful artwork on it to direct the chi toward the other rooms.
7	Keep your pet in another room when company arrives, because if your **dog** jumps on people or scares visitors when they enter, it symbolizes struggling with relationships and scaring off love.

MARCH

8	If you work in a **cubicle**, place a plant near the entrance to mark the boundary of your space.
9	Place **floor lighting** in your office so it comes over the shoulder of your non-dominant hand or it will cast a shadow on your career.
10	To cure the **draining effect** of a bathroom located in the center of the house, place a ceramic bowl (Earth Element) in the room to balance the overabundance of water.
11	If you have **trouble sleeping**, remove the piles of laundry from your bedroom, since these sleep-stealers can make you think more about work than sleep.
12	Position your desk with a wall **behind your back** to ensure that you are supported in your career; if you must sit with your back to a window, make sure there are window coverings.
13	If you want to **travel**, keep books, magazines, and literature about the places you want to visit in your Helpful People area.
14	Clean up **pet waste** in your yard because if you live in a house surrounded by poop, poop is what you attract into your life.

MARCH

15	Clear the **piles of paper** off your desk each night because they symbolize obstruction and keep the prosperity chi from reaching you.
16	Avoid keeping **shoes** out in the open near your front door because they represent walking away from a peaceful life at home.
17	Wear something **green** today, not just because it is St. Patrick's Day, but also because it is the color of the Wood Element that stimulates creativity and growth.
18	**Unfinished projects** represent issues you are trying to avoid; finish them or discard them so you can move on.
19	Remove **unframed mirrors** because their rough edges reflect rough patches in your life; replace them with mirrors framed in wood or metal.
20	Replace your desk if it is not the **right size**: a desk too small for the work to be done makes you feel that your aspirations are restricted; a desk too large will make you feel you are not up to the challenge of the work.
21	Negative chi accumulates after an **illness**, so clean your home thoroughly and leave the windows open for a while after you recover from a cold or flu.

MARCH

22	Hang a **bulletin board** over your child's desk to display awards, artwork, report cards, and great papers to encourage your child to study and achieve.
23	Drape a scarf over the **corners** of dressers and night tables if they point at you in bed because their sharp energy can pierce your sleep.
24	Weed out your home bookshelves, then set up a **library area** in the break room at work to swap books you and your colleagues bring from home.
25	Check to see where your **mirrors** are hung because they increase what they reflect; a mirror across from a pile of unpaid bills will double your debt, but a mirror across from a family vacation photo will double family happiness.
26	Keep your **fish tank** or aquarium clean since a dirty tank clouds your financial future.
27	Remove broken or **cracked mirrors** because they represent fragmentation in your life.
28	Check to make sure artwork that shows a **river** or water is placed so water flows into your home rather than out, retaining wealth in your house rather than draining it out.

FENG SHUI QUICK GUIDE FOR HOME AND OFFICE

MARCH

29	Clean your **garage** because if it is filled with objects you don't need, don't want, or don't use, it sends a message of neglect for your surroundings.
30	Remove any indoor plants that have **spikes or thorns** since they can cause arguments.
31	If you run a home-based business, be sure your work area does not face a **wall** because this blocks your ability to attract clients.

SUCCESS STORY:

Betty's Furniture Studio

Betty's business of designing high-end furniture was good, but she wanted it to be better. Her studio space was L-shaped and, consequently, was missing the Wealth/Prosperity area. Also, when the office manager sat at her desk to invoice clients, her back was to the door, making her feel unsupported. First, I recommended that Betty complete the missing area of her space by painting a prosperity symbol on the driveway where the building was incomplete, to symbolically anchor her wealth. Next, I recommended that Betty reposition the desk so the office manager was sitting in a power position, facing the door.

Betty wrote:

Within a few weeks of making the changes, our business began to pick up, and now our bank account is fatter than it has ever been in the twenty years I have owned the business. I am able to pay all of my bills early and still have extra money. I am sure my Feng Shui changes were the primary catalyst for change, even though my accountant is skeptical!

APRIL

1	Be a little foolish on April Fool's Day: wear **red underwear** today to activate the adventurous side of your personality.
2	Avoid **planting a tree** directly across from your front door, since it will sap your energy and impede financial progress.
3	At the first sign of **spring**, sweep your deck, patio, or porch to get rid of dead leaves and dust.
4	**Dirty windows** cloud judgment because windows represent the eyes of your home; clean them and you will see the world with clear vision.
5	Repair, remove, or replace any **faulty appliances**, missing light bulbs, or stains on the carpet, since all of these can deplete positive chi.
6	Move your **cleaning products** out of any kitchen cabinets where you store food, since storing them in this location symbolizes cleaning out your good health.
7	Sit in the **power position** at meetings — the seat farthest from the door, facing it on a diagonal rather than in a direct line — and you will take control of the conversation.

APRIL

8	Place your cat's **litter box** in the garage, basement, or bathroom rather than in the kitchen or bedroom where it would symbolically contaminate your health.
9	Hang **bells** on the door of your store, especially shops selling clothes and jewelry, because the sound will attract wealth to your business.
10	Remove the **ashes** of your pet from inside your home, since they represent death and stagnant energy.
11	**Artwork** that is hung too low can pull down your perspective; hang it at eye level or just slightly above to uplift your thoughts.
12	Place images of **turtles** in a bedroom as symbols of good health and longevity.
13	Avoid wearing red (Fire Element) at **Passover or Easter** dinner because this hot color could lead to arguments, especially mixed with the heat of cooking and warmer weather.
14	Passover and Easter meals are about joining together, so avoid seating a husband directly across from a wife, which is known as **confrontational seating**.

APRIL

15	If you paid too much in **taxes** this year, place three valuable coins in the wealth area of your house to help activate the flow of prosperity.
16	Avoid keeping an **aquarium** or fish bowl in the kitchen because the water could symbolically put out the fire in your kitchen and reduce prosperity.
17	Choose **office colors** based on what you need to accomplish: red gives importance, yellow lightens a heavy workload, blue helps concentration, green supports growth and change, and white encourages carefulness.
18	Make sure you are not storing **heavy boxes** on the floor near your desk because they will symbolically weigh down your career or business.
19	If you want to encourage **brainstorming**, seat participants in a circle because this shape encourages them to participate equally since no one sits at the head.
20	Make sure nothing is stored **under your bed** so chi can circulate around you when you sleep; if you must use this space, store only soft, out-of-season clothing.
21	If you have a **cemetery** near your home, hang a small mirror on the outside of your house facing it to deflect any negative energy.

APRIL

22	If you work in an office where there are a lot of **arguments**, place a piece of turquoise on your desk, since this stone is associated with connectedness and security.
23	If you are trying to **sell your home**, pack up five of your most treasured belongings and seal them in a moving box as a symbol you are ready, willing, and able to move on.
24	If you are moving into a **new home** or apartment, clean it thoroughly and open the windows for at least thirty minutes to let out the old chi and clear the way for your own energy.
25	Make sure you are not storing any **sharp objects**, books, or exercise equipment under your bed or you may feel exhausted no matter how much rest you get.
26	If you have nasty **neighbors**, plant orange flowers or shrubs with orange blooms between your houses to encourage conversation and communication between the households.
27	A **skylight** cuts a hole in your roof where the chi can escape; if you must sleep under one, cover it with a translucent shade or curtains that you can close at night.
28	To expand **career success**, add objects to your office in the colors purple (Fire Element) and black (Water Element).

APRIL

29	Begin a habit of keeping the **toilet seat lid** down so you don't symbolically flush your wealth away.
30	Hang artwork showing **mountains** on the wall behind the desk in your office to give support to your career.

Jen's New Love

When I came to do her home consultation, Jen was recovering from a bad breakup and was adamant that she didn't want a man in her life. She had arranged her bedroom in a way that was sending the message that she wanted to be alone. I gave her advice for rearranging that room when she was ready to attract a new love.

Jen wrote

I wanted to update you on a positive change in my life. When you came to my house, you made suggestions to me for my bedroom that related to the intention to have a romantic relationship, and I reluctantly followed them. Within a couple of weeks, a friend set me up with a really nice guy. That made me realize I did want a relationship, so I incorporated even more of your romance suggestions and set the intention to have a relationship. I have since met the most wonderful man I could dream of. We are committed to spending the rest of our lives together. I truly believe that my Feng Shui changes were instrumental to being available for my beloved to come into my life. Watch your mail for the wedding invitation!

MAY

<table>
<tr><td>1</td><td>To stop chi from escaping up the fireplace during the months you don't use it, install glass doors or a screen, or fill the opening with a bushy plant.</td></tr>
<tr><td>2</td><td>If you have something unattractive across the street from your home, hang a convex mirror above the front door to deflect negative energy away from you.</td></tr>
<tr><td>3</td><td>If you are setting up a home office, locate it as far from the bedroom as possible or your work will interfere with your sleep and your love life.</td></tr>
<tr><td>4</td><td>If your children must sleep in bunk beds, make sure there is plenty of space between the top bunk and the ceiling for chi to circulate and avoid illness.</td></tr>
<tr><td>5</td><td>Paint your front door to change the energy coming into your home: red — to attract abundance; blue — to encourage a peaceful life; brown — to increase security; green — to support change.</td></tr>
<tr><td>6</td><td>Have a dinner party tonight, and make it lively by displaying a centerpiece of orange flowers, because this yang color encourages active conversation.</td></tr>
<tr><td>7</td><td>If you must display decorative swords and knives, make sure the blades face outward toward the windows or doors, rather than inward toward furniture and people, as they symbolically cut relationships.</td></tr>
</table>

MAY

8	Placing your **purse** on the floor represents disregard for wealth; instead, begin a habit of hanging it on a chair or use a purse hanger to attach it to a table.
9	Trim large trees that grow over the **top of your house** because when limbs hang over a home, they symbolize issues weighing down on the occupants.
10	Create a **meandering path** to your front door to encourage a flow of good wealth into your home; to give the illusion that a straight path curves, plant bushes and flowers along the sides.
11	The direct **glare of the sun** through a window onto a computer screen can cause eyestrain and headache; to help counter this problem place a decorative object or healthy plant on the windowsill.
12	Move your desk if it is located under a heavy **exposed beam**, since the oppressive energy could cause an accident, illness, or misfortune.
13	Remove dead or **dying plants**, especially near the front door, because they generate negative energy.
14	Fix **leaky faucets** in your home since they symbolize prosperity, wealth, and abundance dripping down the drain.

MAY

15	Plant **pine trees** on your property since they represent longevity; if you live in an apartment grow a pine tree in a container on your patio or balcony.
16	**Neutralize your décor** if you are trying to sell your house: expose the hardwood floors or install beige carpet, paint the walls tan, and take down the wallpaper or borders that could seem like art to a prospective buyer.
17	To keep negative energy from accumulating in your home, choose **trashcans** that are as small as you can live with and empty them frequently.
18	Remove photos of **deceased relatives** and pets from the dining room since they can create health problems if you dine in their presence.
19	Make sure you have no **shelves** over your head in your office because the sharp edge and heavy weight make it difficult for you to think clearly or make decisions.
20	Display your **valuable objects** in the living room, such as crystal, collections, or fine art, to symbolize continued wealth.
21	If you **work from home** but don't have a separate room for your office, screen off your work area with a divider, plants, or floor screen.

MAY

22	Hang art with images of **sailing ships** to represent wealth; just remember to select art where the ship is sailing into, not out of, your home or office.
23	There's a reason **wire hangers** are free: they are flimsy, which leads to sloppy closets and chaotic chi; replace them with wood, plastic, or padded hangers.
24	If you want to **lose weight**, avoid using a red tablecloth or place-mats because the color red stimulates the appetite; instead, choose blue, black, or floral patterns.
25	If your **desk chair** is broken, worn, or dusty, it reflects the state of your career; clean, repair, or replace it.
26	Clean out the **top drawer** of your desk today to make room for new opportunities to flow into your career tomorrow.
27	Empty and clean your refrigerator and **freezer** today because outdated food attracts stagnant energy.
28	If you have an **unattractive column** or pillar in your home, hang a small round mirror on it to make it symbolically disappear.

MAY

29	If your **master bedroom** is located over the kitchen, it can have too much yang energy; decorate it in earthy colors and avoid red, orange, or deep purple, candles, or triangular accents (Fire Element).
30	Get rid of items from a **former marriage** or failed relationship because symbolically you will continue to confront that person every time you see the objects.
31	Hang a mirror in a **dark room** to attract light; use any shape except convex, which would deflect the light back to its source rather than attract it into the room.

Karl's Collections

Karl suffered from a condition that is common among many of my clients when it comes to collections: he had too much of a good thing. Karl's impressive music collection included records, CDs, and music-related objects that overflowed his space and dominated his life. His challenge was to move out much of the music he had collected so his music room supported his hobby rather than overpowering him. And then there was his collection of 1,300 beer bottles that he had been keeping since college.

Karl wrote:

I cleared clutter for a few days, then slacked off from your recommended twenty minutes per day. Even such a short period can be hard at first, but I am making progress. I already have many potential outlets for the excess music and I am culling the 200+ CDs. Every time I delve a little deeper, I pull out more to give/sell/toss. I am planning a trip to the local audio shop to consign two sets of speakers. I believe I have found a permanent home for the beer bottles at an expanding brewery out of town. Good excuse to take a road trip!

JUNE

1 Trim **bushes** covering your windows as they block opportunities from reaching you.

2 Make sure there are no prickly plants like **cactus** in front of your house because they have negative chi; if you must keep them, plant fragrant bushes and flowers around them.

3 If your **stove and sink** are directly across from each other, place something green between them — such as a rug — to prevent family arguments and conflict.

4 Paint the inside of your garage a bright, **welcoming color** and hang artwork, such as posters or children's drawings, to welcome you home as soon as you get out of your car.

5 When you are staying in a **hotel**, try to get a room with a water view or view of a curving roadway because the flow of good chi will help you have a smooth and happy trip.

6 To create harmony in a **blended family**, take a family photo of everyone and place a framed copy in your children's rooms; choose a wood frame to encourage family growth.

7 If you want to **attract wealth**, display the following stones in the wealth area of your home: malachite, citrine, lapis, and peridot.

JUNE

8	If you live in an **apartment or condo**, make sure you activate chi in your outdoor space by including a pot of red geraniums, wind chime, mobile, or bird feeder on your patio or balcony.
9	If you are buying a house, avoid selecting one with either rapidly rushing or **stagnant water** behind it; rapid water symbolically carries away a family's prosperity, while stagnant water symbolizes disease and health problems.
10	**Paint** the door between the garage and house the same color as your front door and use the same doormat as in front of the house to provide a warm welcome home no matter which door you enter.
11	Clean out your **wallet**, because a messy wallet symbolizes disregard for your wealth.
12	Make sure the **lighting in your garage** is bright so your return home every night will be equally bright and upbeat.
13	To encourage a happy and **long marriage**, decorate with the colors green (Wood Element) and purple (Fire Element).
14	Remove a **mirrored headboard** since it can interfere with a peaceful night's rest and adversely affect health; if you can't remove the mirror, cover it with a picture of something restful, or drape it with a cloth at night.

JUNE

15	If you want to feel **sophisticated** today, wear luxurious fabrics and metal jewelry and accents (Metal Element).
16	If you are sleeping under a **sloped ceiling** it can cause imbalance or headaches; if you can't move the bed, place tall objects like plants, furniture, or floor lamps in the corners of the room to symbolically raise the ceiling.
17	Create a habit of emptying your **office trashcan** daily because trash represents activities from the past that no longer support your career.
18	Place a pair of matching planters or ceramic pots on either side of your front door to act as a **threshold** to usher positive energy into your home; fill them with bright red flowers.
19	Treat the **garage floor** like you do the other rooms in your home: sweep the dirt out toward the door to keep positive chi flowing.
20	At **mid-year**, conduct a walk-through of your home to make sure your Feng Shui adjustments are still in place; readjust where necessary to help recharge your space to ensure prosperity for the second half of the year.
21	Relocate your **trashcans** outside of your home, or if you must keep them in the garage, empty them frequently.

JUNE

22	If you sleep with your head near a wall that has a **toilet** on the other side, use a thickly padded headboard or hang a quilt or rug on the wall to protect you from the negative chi.
23	Clear out a **file drawer** and shred unnecessary documents; not only will you reduce your risk of identity theft, but you will also symbolically make room for new clients or business to find you.
24	If you have an **unattractive view** of a rooftop, chimney, or corner of a building, hang a small mirror in the window facing the ugly site to push away the negative energy.
25	For a **good night's sleep**, place no more than one mirror in your bedroom and make sure you cannot see yourself in it from the bed.
26	Avoid placing a **shelf overhanging** your bed because its sharp edges will cut your sleep; if you must sleep under a shelf, make sure you keep only soft objects on it.
27	Remove any **exercise equipment** from your bedroom because it has too much yang energy and can result in over-stimulation and sleepless nights.
28	If you live near **power lines** or cell towers, plant tall trees and shrubs around your property to shield you from any negative effects on your health and well-being.

JUNE

29	Avoid having light bulbs directly **above your bed** as they could generate too much chi and make sleep difficult.
30	If you have a **fountain** in your house, make sure it is placed so the water flow is aimed in — not out — of the house so wealth doesn't leave your home.

Erica and Michael's Home Sale

Erica and Michael were moving out of town because of a job change, but their house wasn't selling. They had done all the usual things, including repainting, freshening up the landscaping, and clearing clutter from the closets and garage, but they had no offers — until they made a few simple Feng Shui changes.

Erica and Michael wrote:

As you recommended, we placed a fresh, earth color doormat in front of the main door and a pair of clay pots with red flowers on either side of the door to welcome buyers. The house number was written out in script and couldn't be seen from the street so we replaced it with large black numerals. We boxed up our abstract art as a symbol that we were ready and willing to move, and replaced it with colorful posters with happy family themes. We removed the runner between the front and back doors that was acting like an arrow directing the chi out of the house, and placed large evergreen trees in red planters outside on the pool deck to keep prosperity from dumping into the pool. The result of these simple changes was a contract for full price.

JULY

1	When you go on **vacation**, set timers to turn on lights and create active energy since an empty house can draw negative energies, like burglars, to it.
2	Since your **deck or porch** is part of your home, choose high-quality outdoor furniture and keep it in good condition in all seasons.
3	If your home décor colors are **too hot** for summer, add cool accents like light blue or pale green bedspreads, pillows, or tablecloths to calm and soothe.
4	To balance the yang festivities of fireworks, noise, and sun on the **Fourth of July**, schedule some yin activities that are quiet, sheltered, and intimate to avoid sensory overload.
5	The corkscrew energy of a **ceiling fan** directly over your bed could cause pain or illness; hang a crystal from the pull chain to balance its cutting force.
6	Avoid keeping **work-related objects** in your bedroom; if you must work where you sleep, use a curtain, floor screen, or plants to hide your work after you finish for the day.
7	Even if you prefer using a microwave or barbecue grill in hot weather, use your **stove** occasionally, because an unused stove implies untapped resources or ignored opportunities.

JULY

8	Keep your pets off **furniture**, especially the chairs and tables, or your animals will dominate your household.
9	If you have a **tree stump** near your house, invigorate the dead energy by planting ivy or other plants around it that will cover the stump, or display a brightly colored planter on top of it.
10	If you have **open staircases**, which represent a hole in your home, place tall, bushy plants under the stairs or pictures of trees and flowers on the wall to ground the area.
11	Remove any vines growing on your house because, while the image of an **ivy-covered** cottage may be romantic, vines on your home symbolize something eating away at your life.
12	Keep your **garden** fresh, natural, and flowing: deadhead flowers when they fade but avoid over-pruning your trees and shrubs into tight shapes.
13	If your new opportunities have slowed, be sure your **doorbell** works so that opportunity can come calling.
14	Clear the **path** to your front door and repair any cracks, or negative energy will symbolically "trip you up" and make it difficult to achieve your goals.

JULY

15	To ward off **intruders** while you are on vacation, set a radio to a talk station and put it on a timer so you will have conversation in your home, which creates active yang energy.
16	To help your baby sleep, position the head of the **crib** against a wall, just as you would a regular bed.
17	If you need to feel **grounded** at work today, wear brown or yellow clothes to represent the Earth Element.
18	Make sure you are not **storing shoes** under the bed, especially if you have trouble sleeping, since they represent "walking away" from peaceful rest.
19	Buy a new bed after a **divorce** because when you sleep on a mattress or frame from a failed relationship, you are sleeping with your past — and with your former spouse.
20	If your **laundry room** is in the center of your home, prosperity could be draining out of your life; add brown or yellow objects to represent the Earth Element and absorb excess water.
21	Clean your **office windows** or you will be looking at your career through a dirty lens.

JULY

22	Avoid hanging a mirror on the wall directly across from the front door because it will **reflect the chi** back out the door rather than invite it into your home.
23	Fix all loose **doorknobs**, especially in your wealth area, because they can make it difficult to "get a grip" on your financial situation.
24	If you have a job **interview**, audition, or important meeting, wear something red — like a tie or jewelry — to activate the Fire Element and ignite your personal power.
25	Choose the auspicious **number nine** whenever you can, such as in your ATM password or personalized license plates, and it will invite prosperity and wealth into your life.
26	If you want to **attract wealth**, surround yourself with pictures of things that feel wealthy and prosperous to you, like a Mercedes, a Malibu beach house, or a money pile.
27	Ask a good friend to give you an honest opinion of whether your home smells from **pet odors**, and take care of the problem immediately.
28	Place the **head of your bed** against a wall or solid support and you will get a good night's sleep.

JULY

29	Hang a mirror in your **foyer** on the right hand side as you enter the house to attract opportunities into your life.
30	To set your **perspective** for the day, hang an upbeat piece of art across from your bed, because it is the first thing you will see each morning.
31	**Clear out** one closet, one drawer, and one cabinet today, then step back and watch what new things flow into your life to fill the empty spaces you have created.

Marcia's Home Business

My client Marcia had made changes to her expanding home business that not only increased her revenue but also resulted in the manifestation of the perfect office space outside of her home when she wasn't even looking for it. She loved her leased office space but missed the convenience of working at home.

Marcia wrote:

There was a miracle. I had been wanting to purchase a home for twelve years, but everything seemed to be too expensive, in the wrong area of town, have no landscaping, or need too much fixing up. Then, I found a house listed in the newspaper. It had already been sold, but the buyers couldn't come up with the money so they re-listed it. As soon as I walked into the yard and looked in the windows I knew it was my new home. And because the sellers had reduced the price I had the exact amount for a down payment. The house has a separate studio with high ceilings and large windows — you guessed it, the perfect location to move my business back home. I really feel that the Feng Shui changes in my previous house started freeing up energy and guided me to this home.

AUGUST

1 If your back yard **slopes** away from your home, plant tall, straight plants or build a wall to keep the chi from running out of your life.

2 If your front door faces a stairway, hang a **crystal chandelier** or cut glass light fixture in the foyer to keep the energy from running directly up to the next level.

3 When the light bulbs outside your front door burn out, replace them immediately because they represent **burnt out energy** for people living in the home.

4 Make sure your bed has a **headboard**, because sleeping without one, or with one that is loose or unstable, can make you feel insecure and unsupported in life.

5 Remove all items hanging on the **back of doors**; doors represent opportunities so the extra weight represents more struggles in your life.

6 If your front door faces a tall building or a **telephone pole**, plant a few tall bushes to block this poison arrow chi from hitting your house.

7 If you have a **squeaky garage door**, fix it since it represents stuck energy in the area of the bagua that it occupies.

AUGUST

8	The number eight is especially auspicious, so on this eighth day of the eighth month, display a figure-eight-shaped **gourd** at your dinner table to symbolize good health and long life for the entire family.
9	Add a fish tank or aquarium to your home office as a symbol of activity; a tank with **nine fish** is considered the best combination to bring wealth into a home (eight gold and one black).
10	If you just **moved** into your house, make sure the pathway to the front door is clear so the positive energy can find you at your new location.
11	If you enter your home through the **utility room**, paint and decorate it to look like a foyer so your life will not feel too utilitarian.
12	If you feel you have **too much to do** every day, place a collection of river stones in a bowl near your front door to "hold down" worries.
13	To correct a missing bagua area of your apartment or condo, hang a flat, **rectangular mirror** on a wall you need to symbolically move out.
14	**Conserve water** and avoid letting it run down the drain unnecessarily, as it represents abundance and wealth.

FENG SHUI QUICK GUIDE FOR HOME AND OFFICE

AUGUST

15 Remove furniture and clutter from **hallways** so chi can flow unimpeded.

16 If you have had an accident or a **traumatic experience**, surround yourself with the color brown because it has a grounding effect.

17 Remove any objects that you never use from your **basement** to keep healthy energy circulating underneath you and give you a strong, supportive foundation.

18 Discard torn and **stained** items in your office since they represent disregard for your work and clients and block the flow of new business.

19 To create family harmony, choose furniture with **rounded edges** rather than sharp corners or angles.

20 Position your bed so you can see the **entrance to the room** when you are in it to give you a restful, secure feeling and encourage sleep.

21 To increase **cash flow** for your business, place three valuable coins on your telephone, on top of your computer, in the cash register, or in a critical client file.

AUGUST

22	If you are an author struggling with **writer's block**, surround yourself with objects in the colors blue (Water Element) or green (Wood Element) for inspiration and growth.
23	If you want to encourage **harmony and abundance**, surround yourself with objects in the color combination of red (Fire Element) and gold (Metal Element).
24	If your driveway has a **slope**, install a light or reflectors at the top of it to stop the drain of wealth away from the house.
25	Play **music** to add yang energy to your house, but choose carefully: rock music stimulates desire; country music stimulates emotions; classical music provides inspiration.
26	Remove **dead bugs** from around your house because they represent stagnant energy surrounding your life.
27	**Dried flowers** symbolize dead energy; remove them from your home and office and replace them with fresh, seasonal flowers.
28	Clear **clutter** from the Wealth area of your home to avoid stagnation and open up space for wealth to flow into your life.

AUGUST

29	To counteract **sharp corners** from walls or furniture aimed at you in your workplace, place healthy plants with soft, rounded leaves in front of them.
30	Place **biographies** of people you admire or inspirational books in the Career area of your home to increase your work success.
31	Place a **palm plant** in your office because it is especially good at removing toxic substances like formaldehyde from carpeting and furniture.

Jacob's L-Shaped House

Jacob lived in an L-shaped house that was missing the Helpful People/Mentors area. His business was failing because his competitors were stealing his ideas. Jacob longed to restart a career in academia but didn't know how to make it happen. I recommended he restore the missing area of his home by placing three small rocks in the front corner to anchor it.

Jacob wrote:

My wife and I had a fun trip to the lake, where we collected rocks to anchor the missing area of our house. The following week the most amazing thing happened. A friend who worked at the local community college called to give me a heads up about a new position being created, working for a person I knew. When I called, the person admitted he wouldn't have thought of me for the job — but that I was perfect. I had two easy interviews, and he offered me the job. I would have never found out about the job if my friend and mentor hadn't called me about it. I am convinced that filling in the Mentor area of our home made the difference.

SEPTEMBER

1	To attract new opportunities year round, change your **doormat** at the beginning of every new season.
2	To get ahead of **school paper** clutter early in the school year, create a space for the homework, books, and notices that children bring home from school.
3	If you want your children to **study** in their rooms instead of at the kitchen table or in front of the TV, add a desk to their bedroom; children who have a place to study, study.
4	Keep your **appointment book** or PDA in the lower right hand corner of your desk, which is the Helpful People area that attracts clients and mentors to your life.
5	If the **mudroom** is the first room in your home that you see upon entering, avoid storing old, broken furniture and unneeded items in this area so your life will not feel second-hand.
6	To enhance your relationship with your **spouse**, hang a romantic picture in your bedroom that shows a couple holding hands.
7	To help young children learn to **hang up their clothes**, remove their closet doors, lower rods, and buy child-sized hangers.

SEPTEMBER

8	Place **photos of parents**, grandparents, and happy family gatherings in children's bedrooms to help communicate love and security and help them sleep.
9	If you want to stimulate your **children's creativity**, add white and metallic colors and objects (Metal Element) to their rooms.
10	Avoid hanging a mirror in your **children's rooms**, especially if they aren't sleeping well; if your child must have a mirror, hang it on the inside of the closet door and close the door at night.
11	To help your children succeed in school, place these objects in their rooms: a **globe** to encourage curiosity, a map to ground them, and charts of the stars and planets to expand horizons.
12	Place an aquarium in your child's room as a symbol of **educational success** and to encourage responsibility.
13	If your **child** isn't sleeping well, remove anything stored under the bed to allow energy to flow and encourage sleep.
14	Clean your **dorm room** windows to let in the maximum amount of light and illuminate your studies.

FENG SHUI QUICK GUIDE FOR HOME AND OFFICE

SEPTEMBER

15	Make sure your **house number** is clearly visible from the street, both during the day and at night, so positive chi can find you.
16	Things stored in an **attic** weigh down on you; remove anything that you don't need or that has negative associations to lift burdens off your shoulders.
17	Avoid hanging pictures of **wild animals** at the top of the stairs because they can be too scary and keep the chi from flowing to the next level of your house.
18	Overhead **fluorescent** lights represent sharp Metal Element energy stabbing you in the head; turn them off and substitute a desk and floor lamp for more gentle lighting.
19	Remove **caged pets** from your child's room because their activity discourages sleep; if that is the only place for them, make sure the cage is kept clean, the pet is healthy, and cover the cage at night if you can.
20	**Mirrored closet doors** interfere with peaceful sleep; replace them with solid doors or hang a drape above the closet to tie back during the day and close when you go to sleep at night.
21	If you **share an office**, avoid placing the desks across from each other to prevent "head-to-head" confrontations.

SEPTEMBER

22	Pull up dead summer annuals and cut back perennials in the garden because they represent **stale chi**; replace them with colorful mums or hardy pansies that will give you active chi until the first frost.
23	Remove any mirror at the end of a **long hallway**, especially where it reflects an unattractive view, because the chi will bounce straight back down the hall and not enter the rooms.
24	If you need to make a **decision** at a meeting, seat participants at a rectangular table because there are fewer verbal exchanges when people sit side by side, so conversations will be to the point.
25	Place a living plant within three feet of your **computer** to help clean the air in your office.
26	Avoid placing a **baby's crib** in direct line with the door; the strong flow of energy entering a room is too harsh for a little one to handle.
27	Display a bowl of fruit or a cookie jar on your **dining room** table; symbolically your table will never be empty and you can always nourish your family.
28	Display a rooster image in your office to keep down office politicking and **gossip**, and enhance your own reputation.

SEPTEMBER

29	**Fix** anything that isn't working in your home and you will fix what is broken in your life.
30	Instead of saving every art piece your child brings home, take **digital photos** of it so you can watch it as a slide show whenever you want.

Clara's Barter

When Clara launched her consulting practice, her first client, an artist, paid her with an original lithograph instead of a check. They had agreed on a fee up front, but after the work was done the client asked if Clara would consider a barter because her funds were limited. Clara took the beautiful print but kept it rolled up in a tube in her closet, feeling that she sold her services short. When she called me for a consultation three months later, her business was going nowhere. I reminded her that the print was valuable and that she obviously liked it or she wouldn't have accepted it, but by keeping it stashed away in the closet she was symbolically reducing the value of both her services and her client's talent.

Clara wrote:

I took your advice and had the print professionally framed. I hung it in my office, where I could see it every day. The result was an immediate increase in calls from prospective clients — and these clients paid in cash. I am now experiencing a dramatic improvement in cash flow because of this simple Feng Shui change. I do love the piece and feel better about the barter every day.

OCTOBER

1 Clear the **cobwebs** from your outdoor furniture before you cover it for the winter; accumulated cobwebs symbolize being so wrapped up and stuck that you can't move forward.

2 Even if the weather outside is chilly, **open your windows** today, and occasionally during the fall and winter months, to let in some fresh air and fresh chi energy.

3 Remove **dead leaves** from your gutters and roof since they represent dead chi accumulating on top of your home.

4 **Hang plants** in your bathrooms because they represent the Wood Element that helps counteract negative aspects of the waste in this room.

5 Avoid using red as the **dominant color** in the kitchen because there is already enough of the Fire Element from the stove and microwave.

6 In your office, position your desk so you can **face the doorway**; if you must sit with your back to the door, place a small mirror so you can see who is entering the space.

7 **Rearrange furniture** today; even if you only move the sofa a few inches closer to the window or the lamp to a different side of the table, it will bring new energy into your room.

OCTOBER

8 Remove **tall furniture** that is close to the bed in a child's room because it can feel like a towering cliff to a young child.

9 If you have a **leaky toilet**, fix it immediately because leaking water represents leaking wealth.

10 Avoid having your company name or logo on your **welcome mat** because it symbolizes people "walking all over" your reputation.

11 Place a vase of fresh flowers in your bedroom when you are trying to recover from an **illness**.

12 Avoid keeping **mops and brooms** out in the open in the kitchen or storing them in the pantry because this symbolizes sweeping out your nutrition and health.

13 If you live in a house located on a **T-junction**, the traffic aimed at your house acts like a sharp arrow creating hostility in the house; hang a wind chime or plant shrubs in front of your house to deflect the negative energy.

14 Paint your bedroom a **skin tone color** to encourage sleep; avoid white or icy colors because they are too cold and can make you restless at night.

OCTOBER

15 When you **clear clutter** and can't decide whether to keep an item, ask yourself whether you would pay a mover to move the item; the answer will help you decide whether to keep or toss it.

16 If you want to **change jobs**, place inspirational books and self-help manuals related to your career field in the Career area of your home and office.

17 If you have to keep **stacks of files** on your desk, place them to your side rather than pile them in front of you, where they represent obstacles blocking career success.

18 Remove **clutter from your car**; cars move us forward so a clean one invites opportunities to move forward in your life.

19 When you **repair an object** and it feels like a treasure has been restored, keep it; but if you look at a repaired object and see only damage, get rid of it.

20 Place your **office phone** on top of a red cloth, paper, or pad to bring in more calls and more clients.

21 If the only location for your bed is **underneath a window**, make sure you have curtains or shutters on the windows and keep them closed while sleeping.

OCTOBER

22	If you inherit a **valuable heirloom** but dislike the person you inherited it from, it represents negative energy; sell or donate the object rather than display it.
23	Add green accents to your **family room** to symbolize family growth; to reduce arguments, avoid high-energy colors like red and orange in this room.
24	If you have something in your closet that you haven't used in over a year, get rid of it, then watch something unexpected **fill the space** you have opened up.
25	Clear unnecessary files from your **hard drive** to make room for new projects, clients, customers, and ideas.
26	If you live in a house at the end of a **cul-de-sac**, the energy can go around the curve like a slingshot, making the house feel cold and isolated; hang wind chimes by your door or plant colorful flowers out front to encourage the chi to stop at your home.
27	If you see the **toilet** from your bed, keep the bathroom door closed at night to facilitate sleep.
28	If you want to **meet new friends** and have a more active social life, surround yourself with pictures of happy occasions and smiling people.

FENG SHUI QUICK GUIDE FOR HOME AND OFFICE

OCTOBER

29	To increase **creativity**, clear the clutter from the top of your workspace and from inside your desk drawers.
30	Arrange your **sofa and chairs** so you can see the main door into the room and you will feel secure; if you must sit with your back to a door, place a table behind you for protection.
31	It's fun to wear a **mask** for Halloween, but remove masks from the wall, especially in a bedroom, because they represent hiding or covering up something.

Wendy's Home Office

When I visited Wendy's home for a consultation, I immediately realized that the dark basement was the wrong location for her growing home-based marketing business. I recommended that she instead locate the business in the upstairs guest room, which was little used. I was delighted when Wendy sent me a photo of her fabulous new home office that she had relocated. She not only ended up with a more functional, brighter office, but also got an unexpected bonus.

Wendy wrote:

I moved my office upstairs and am convinced that move helped lead to the launch of my new website, among other things. And, as you suggested, I also began mailing things in red envelopes to encourage some prosperity for my business. Now I am going to be on HGTV! I wrote about moving my office on my blog, and someone at the station noticed it. They redecorated the basement room that used to be my office, which I made into the guest bedroom, for a show called "FreeStyle" about transforming existing rooms. It was exciting to have them come over. And my business benefited from the national exposure.

NOVEMBER

1 Hang a mirror that reflects your dining room table and you will symbolically double your wealth because **entertaining guests** is associated with prosperity.

2 Resist the urge to display **seashells** or use water images or the color blue in the bath because there is already enough of the Water Element in this room; instead decorate in earth-tone colors.

3 Keep **photos of your children** in rooms where people gather to visibly represent the joy that has resulted from your happy relationship.

4 If your kitchen is near your front door, it may encourage **over-eating**; keep the kitchen door closed or hang a mirror or artwork near the kitchen entrance to distract your eye from the room.

5 Burn **scented candles** in your home to change your perspective: vanilla to make a room feel comforting, peppermint to curb your appetite, strawberry to boost energy and make you want to exercise, a floral fragrance to enhance learning, pine to enhance well-being.

6 Keep your **fountain** flowing because if it goes dry, it represents a drain of prosperity, especially if it is located by the front door.

7 Clear your **computer desktop** because clutter there has the same negative effect on your career as a messy desk, blocking productivity and success; add a screen saver of a river to encourage the flow of creativity.

NOVEMBER

8	Keep your **refrigerator** well stocked because a full fridge symbolizes abundance, opulence, and generosity.
9	Start a **new habit**: when you change your clocks back to standard time and replace the batteries in your smoke detectors, clean your refrigerator and pantry and toss expired foods and old spices.
10	If your clutter includes **magazines** that you don't have time to read, cancel your subscriptions; read them online if possible.
11	On Veterans Day and all year long, if your loved one is **deployed** overseas, display two photos of him or her in your Family/Community area—one in uniform and another in civilian clothes — to symbolize a safe and speedy return home.
12	Bring Mother Nature indoors by using **full-spectrum** light bulbs that simulate daylight, especially in the winter months; install dimmers to control lighting throughout the year.
13	Reduce the number of **old family photos** you display since they can represent living in the past and the inability to move forward; display at least one current photo of every family member.
14	The **dining room** is considered to be a place of wealth, so use it frequently instead of always eating in front of the TV, especially during the holiday season.

15 Keep **recycling bins** far away from your door because they contain unwanted items that represent negative chi.

16 **Dust your office** frequently since accumulated dust represents a lack of respect for what is going on in your career.

17 Avoid **clutter in the kitchen**, which creates stagnant energy that interferes with your ability to cook and enjoy healthy, nourishing food.

18 Seat a **guest of honor** across from one spouse and seat the other spouse in the middle, complementary position to encourage the flow of conversation.

19 If you invite a **special companion** for dinner, position your guest facing away from the kitchen, a power position that will make him or her feel important.

20 Choose a **rectangular table** for your dining room because it represents the Wood Element that can grow infinitely, which symbolically allows an unlimited number of guests to join the table.

21 Plan **Thanksgiving decorations** based on the meaning of their colors and shapes: squares for unity, circles for lively conversation, and the color orange for connection.

NOVEMBER

22	Display a Thanksgiving **centerpiece** of fresh fruit and vegetables to represent good health and longevity.
23	If you have mirrors hung so they face each other, they could contribute to **arguments**; remove or relocate one of them.
24	Before a holiday meal is a good time to remove any **chipped** plates or glassware from your kitchen because such items represent negative energy.
25	If you have a **bookshelf headboard**, replace it because the edges could contribute to headaches; plus, too many books behind your head can stimulate your mind and cause insomnia.
26	**Sweep the kitchen floor** toward the door, to symbolically sweep out the old negative energy and make room for good health.
27	Used **mattresses**, sleep sofas, and futons hold the energy of their former owners, so avoid bringing a bed into your home if you don't know who slept on it or you could be sleeping with all of their issues.
28	When you arrive home after a **trip**, open the windows for a short while, run the water, and use your stove so fresh chi can begin to circulate immediately.

NOVEMBER

29	Keep one-quarter of your **storage area** unused to encourage new ideas, relationships, and opportunities to flow your way.
30	If you have **bookshelves** directly behind you in your office, move them because their sharp edges symbolize confrontation or backstabbing.

SUCCESS STORY:
Karen's Feng Shui Party

I gave Karen a list of Feng Shui changes for her home, and she made them all at once by inviting a group of friends to help her move furniture and hang art. She hired two people to do the heavy lifting; and she provided food, drink, and music, which made the process seem easier and more enjoyable for all involved. The result was a fun evening and a gorgeous makeover that has already made a big difference in her life.

Karen wrote:

Having my space come together like that all at once was so good for my life. I am just being taken care of: things are flowing into my life from old connections and from heaven above. I am completing tasks now because my space is clear. And what fun having my friends become part of this process of transformation. Feng Shui really works.

DECEMBER

1 Locate your **Christmas tree** in the Wealth area because triangular shapes displayed in this area enhance finances.

2 Make sure the **burners** on your stove are in good working condition because they symbolize wealth; immediately fix any nonworking burners.

3 Choose a **holiday tablecloth** in a color that represents prosperity for your guests, such as red or green with metallic accents.

4 Avoid using all of your holiday **decorations** this year; vary what you display each year to make each object more meaningful.

5 If you don't put up a Christmas tree, bring a bit of **nature** indoors by displaying evergreen boughs or poinsettias to counteract winter gloom and encourage guests to laugh and mingle.

6 Avoid giving **bonsai trees** and other stunted plants as gifts since they symbolize limited growth.

7 Give full, healthy plants with **rounded leaves** as gifts because they send a message of prosperity and long life to the recipient.

DECEMBER

8	Give gifts of **jade** to wish someone good health and longevity.
9	Avoid giving sharp objects like **knives**, scissors, letter openers, or can openers as gifts since they represent cutting a relationship; if you receive one of these as a gift, hand over a penny to symbolically restore the bond between you and the giver.
10	Avoid giving an **empty wallet**, purse, or briefcase as a gift; instead, fill it with dollar coins or bills to send the message that your gift will always be overflowing with wealth for the recipient.
11	Avoid giving plants with sharp, pointed leaves or thorns as gifts since they symbolize a **thorny friendship.**
12	Avoid giving **handkerchiefs** because they symbolize wiping away tears and suggest that you expect the recipient to be doing a lot of crying in the future.
13	Avoid giving **watches and clocks** as gifts since they symbolize stealing it from others; instead, give a gift certificate along with a picture of a watch.
14	**Re-gifting** is positive because it removes unwanted things from your home, but avoid re-gifting if you have negative feelings about the original giver since you could pass these on to the next recipient.

DECEMBER

15 No matter how valuable the **art**, avoid purchasing something with a depressing or negative theme because it can pull down the positive chi energy in your home.

16 If you stand with your back to the doorway when you are at the **kitchen sink**, you can symbolically be caught off guard; place a small mirror in front of you so you can see what is going on behind your back.

17 Maintain harmony during the **holiday season** by balancing yin and yang in your decorating and using opposites in your color scheme — dark and light, hard and soft, active and passive.

18 If you need to improve a family member's **health** during the holiday season, decorate with twinkling lights or ornaments around the center of your home or room (the Grounding/Balance area).

19 If you celebrate **Hanukkah**, decorate in the traditional colors of blue (Water Element) to make your holiday flow smoothly, and silver (Metal Element) for strength.

20 To increase your **prosperity**, display a crystal bowl of chocolate Hanukkah gelt (money) and the holiday gifts you have received in the Wealth area of your home.

21 Play **relaxing music** during the holidays, shut off the TV, and keep the entertainment center doors closed to encourage better communication among family and friends.

DECEMBER

22	Avoid seating an **overbearing guest** at the head of the table where he or she could monopolize the conversation; instead seat the guest on the side of the table to blend in better.
23	If your family is prone to **squabbles** during the holiday season, invite an even number of guests, keep the lights low and soft, and decorate with soothing earth tones like gold, green, and brown.
24	If you have annoying relatives at your holiday diner, seat them **nearest to the door**, because whoever is seated near the door is usually the first one to leave.
25	Serve **Christmas dinner** on the good china, crystal, and silver you have been hiding in your cabinets and closets, because negative chi accumulates in things you don't use frequently.
26	Keep the **lights on** at the front of your house to increase your opportunities for recognition, especially during the holiday season.
27	To add **warmth to your home** during winter, add warm colors in the form of a fresh or silk flower arrangement, throw pillows, and afghans.
28	If you suffer from the **winter blues**, especially around the holidays, counteract feelings of loneliness by surrounding yourself with the color orange and avoiding use of the color blue.

DECEMBER

29	Get rid of **clothes** you didn't wear during the year; holding on to clothes that are the wrong size or style symbolizes holding on to old behavior patterns.
30	After **taking down the tree**, weed out the decorations you no longer like and the lights you no longer use, and recycle them.
31	Decorate your home for **New Year's Eve** with gold and silver, the colors of valuable coins, symbolizing your intention to attract wealth in the coming year.

PART FIVE

Appendices

APPENDIX
1

BIBLIOGRAPHY

Clutter and Space Clearing

Carter, Karen Rauch, *Move Your Stuff, Change Your Life: How to Use Feng Shui to Get Love, Money, Respect and Happiness.* New York, NY : Simon and Schuster, 2000.

Kingston, Karen, *Clear Your Clutter with Feng Shui.* New York, NY: Broadway Books, 1999.

Linn, Denise, *Sacred Space.* New York, NY: Ballantine Books, 1995.

Walsh, Peter, *Does This Clutter Make My Butt Look Big?: An Easy Plan for Losing Weight and Living More.* New York, NY: Free Press, 2008.

Walsh, Peter, *It's All Too Much: An Easy Plan For Living A Richer Life with Less Stuff*. New York, NY: Free Press, 2007.

Color Theory

Sawahata, Lesa, *Color Harmony Workbook: A Workbook and Guide to Creative Color Combinations*. Gloucester, MA: Rockport Publishers, 1999.

Creativity/Law of Attraction

Arcuri, Mark, *A Life Aligned*. Hallandale, FL: ALA Press, 2008.

Byrne, Rhonda, *The Secret*. New York, NY: Atria Books, 2006.

Cameron, Julia, *The Artist's Way*. New York, NY: Tarcher/Putnum, 1992.

Feng Shui/Art of Placement

Collins, Terah Kathryn, *The Western Guide to Feng Shui*. Carlsbad, CA: Hay House, Inc., 1996.

Gallagher, Winifred, *The Power of Place*. New York, NY: Poseidon Press, 1994.

Saunders, Steven and Simon Brown, *Feng Shui Food*. Guildford, CT: The Lyons Press, 2003.

Silverman, Sherri, *Vastu*. Layton, UT: Gibbs Smith, 2007.

Wydra, Nancilee, *Feng Shui in the Garden: Simple Solutions for Creating Comforting, Life-Affirming Gardens of the Soul*. Chicago, IL: Contemporary Books, 1997.

RESOURCES

Are you intrigued by Feng Shui and want more information? Check out these additional resources:

Links

Visit my website, *www.FengShuiForRealLife.com*, for additional information about the basics and benefits of Feng Shui. Be sure to go to the *feng shui basics* tab to see full-color versions of the graphics used in this book.

Monthly Feng Shui For Real Life E-zine

The tips in this book provide ample advice to get you started on your path to improving your life. But if this book has you hooked on Feng Shui or you have specific questions, you can get additional help through my free monthly *Feng Shui For Real Life E-zine*. Each month I answer readers' questions plus send you tips, success stories, seasonal advice, articles, and intriguing information that goes beyond Feng Shui.

To subscribe to this e-publication, please register at this link on my website: *http://www.fengshuiforreallife.com/newsletter*.

Clutter Clearing Help

If you have a problem controlling clutter, you're not alone: millions of Americans suffer from chronic hoarding and clutter. To make matters worse, we waste at least 55 minutes a day looking for things, and we never use 80 percent of what we own. If you have successfully completed *The Feng Shui Clutter Clinic* you might be looking at a big pile of stuff right now and wondering what you can do with it. My free tip sheet, *88 Feel-Good Reasons To Get Rid of It*, includes websites for numerous places where you can donate your stuff, take a tax write-off, and feel good while doing it. You can download a copy at: *www.FengShuiForRealLife.com/gifts*.

Also, you can download the e-book *Clutter Free and Clear: Take Charge of Your Time and Space!* at *www.ClutterFreeAndClear.com*. I wrote the chapter on Feng Shui and clutter for this compilation of tips on clutter clearing, including computer clutter, time boundaries, hoarding, events and parties, clutter clearing for aging parents, and clutter clearing in various rooms. Every chapter includes exercises to help you move forward on your clutter-clearing path.

Home, Office, and Business Consultations

I am fortunate to live in two locations, so on a regular basis I schedule consultations in the Northeast (Washington, D.C./Maryland suburbs, Baltimore, Annapolis, New York City, and North Jersey) and the Southwest (Santa Fe, Albuquerque, Los Alamos, Denver, Phoenix).

Nationwide, I do travel frequently so you never know when I am going to be in your state. My travel schedule always appears monthly in the *Feng Shui For Real Life E-zine*, or you can e-mail me directly for details about scheduling a consultation in your location: *carol@FengShuiForRealLife.com*.

Custom Workshops and Keynote Speeches

Feng Shui is a popular topic for breakfast, luncheon, and dinner meetings, special events, fundraisers, business seminars, and college and university training sessions. My Feng Shui workshops are customized to meet the needs of your group or organization. Whether it is a talk at your group dinner, monthly meeting, office staff development session, or holiday luncheon, my Feng Shui presentations are fun and, as fundraisers, always sell out.

Here are some of the most popular topics I present:
- Asian/Pacific American Heritage Month Themes
- Bedroom Feng Shui
- Feng Shui Clutter Clinic
- Feng Shui for Children's Rooms
- Feng Shui Goes to Work

- Feng Shui in the Garden
- Feng Shui, Love, and Relationships
- Feng Shui and The Secret
- Feng Shui Tips for Attracting Wealth
- Home Office Feng Shui
- Introduction to Feng Shui
- Look Twice, Buy Once for Home Buyers
- Sell It Fast with Feng Shui

For more information about scheduling a home or office consultation or a customized workshop for your group, please call 1.800.652.9038.

A SPECIAL BONUS
FROM CAROL OLMSTEAD

To thank you for reading this book, I am happy to provide a free bonus article, *Feng Shui Tips to Help Recession-Proof Your Life*.

Economic downturns can represent a challenge for all of us. The Feng Shui tips in this special article are designed to help keep your wealth flowing and to make your home recession-proof despite a poor economy. To download your copy, please go to *www.FengShuiForRealLife.com/gifts*.

GLOSSARY

This glossary of Feng Shui terms will help clarify some of the concepts discussed in this book. For a more in-depth glossary that includes terminology used by different branches and schools of Feng Shui, please go to *www.internationalfengshuiguild.org,* scroll down, and click on the link for the *International Feng Shui Guild Glossary.*

adjustment
A specific Feng Shui improvement, cure, or remedy recommended by a practitioner to help a client change the energy in a home or office.

auspicious
A term used in Feng Shui to denote favorable, desirable, and beneficial influences and successful results.

bagua

A mapping chart used in Feng Shui analysis of a home or office to divide a space into nine areas related to life attributes. The bagua consists of eight sectors representing aspects of life, and one central one representing balance. Each sector, or gua, relates to a specific Element, color, and shape. The nine areas of the contemporary bagua are: Power/Wealth/Abundance, Fame/Future/Reputation, Love/Marriage/Relationships, Creativity/Children/Legacy, Compassion/Travel/Helpful People, Self/Career/Work, Knowledge/Wisdom/Harmony, Family/Health/Community, Well-Being/Balance.

Pronounced *bag-wha*.

built environment

An interior environment that is the product of design and execution; the opposite of the natural, growing environment outside of homes and buildings.

Certified Feng Shui Practitioner

A Feng Shui practitioner who has achieved a certain level of expertise and who has received a certificate of achievement or completion from a recognized school of Feng Shui.

chi

The vital energy that comes from nature, which is the constantly moving and changing force making us feel either good or bad in a certain location. Every person, object, and environment has the living energy called chi. Chi is always in motion, swirling around people and around the objects that people place in their surroundings. Chi can be positive or negative.

Pronounced *chee*.

clutter
The accumulation of unused, unneeded, and unwanted objects. In Feng Shui, clutter represents postponed decisions and the inability to move forward.

continuity and connectedness
The link between what you see and what you attract into your life. Because every action has a reaction, we are influenced by everything around us and, in turn, we influence everything. Therefore, the colors, shapes, and images used to decorate surroundings will influence what you attract into your life. The more you surround yourself with symbols of what you want to attract into your life, the more likely you are to achieve it.

crystals
Used in Feng Shui as remedies or cures to correct inauspicious situations or to attract positive chi. Objects made of clear, high-quality faceted glass can also be used for this purpose.

cure, *also called remedy or adjustment*
An object, icon, action, affirmation, or intention used to make a Feng Shui change or adjustment in a home or office. Cures are used either to attract positive energy or to eliminate negative or stagnant energy.

Dao

See *Tao*.

Earth Element

One of the Five Elements. Earth is represented by the colors yellow, brown, and earthtones, as well as square shapes. Earth energy relates to stability, balance, and grounding.

electro-magnetic field, *also called EMF*

An energy field produced where electric current is flowing. Overexposure to excessive EMFs is believed to be harmful to health, and Feng Shui adjustments are made to minimize the effects.

Elements

The way colors and shapes are represented in Feng Shui. Each Element governs specific aspects of life, and each is characterized by a specific shape and colors.

See also, *Five Elements*.

energy *also called chi*

The constantly moving and changing force around you, making you feel either good or bad in a certain location. Feng Shui concerns itself with the movement and quality of energy, since creating a healthy and positive flow of energy enhances the quality of life.

feng

The Chinese word for wind.

Pronounced *fung*.

Feng Shui

The art and science of placing things around you in balance and harmony with the natural world. The words translate as *wind* and *water*. Feng Shui is thought to be more than 5,000 years old.

Pronounced *fung shway*.

Feng Shui For Real Life ®

A contemporary, intuitive, and integrative approach to Feng Shui.

Fire Element

One of the Five Elements. Fire is represented by the colors red, purple, magenta, pink, and orange, as well as the triangular shape. Fire energy symbolizes wealth, power, fame, and reputation.

Five Elements

The term to describe the colors, shapes, and textures around you and the attributes they bring into your life. The Five Elements are Fire, Earth, Metal, Water, and Wood. Placement of these Elements affects chi and forms the basis for achieving balance and harmony.

Five Element creation cycle

Refers to the cycle in which each of the Five Elements creates, nourishes, and enhances the subsequent one in the following sequence: Fire *creates* Earth; Earth *yields* Metal; Metal *attracts* Water; Water *feeds* Wood; Wood *fuels* Fire.

Five Element destruction cycle

Refers to the cycle in which each of the elements controls, weakens, or dominates another in the following sequence: Fire *consumes* Wood; Earth *extinguishes* Fire; Metal *cuts* Earth; Water *rusts* Metal; Wood *drinks* Water.

five power principles
The guiding concepts of Feng Shui necessary to achieve balance. The Five Power Principles are: Chi, the Five Elements, the Bagua, Yin and Yang, Continuity and Connectedness.

gua
A sector or area, specifically the sectors of the Feng Shui bagua. The contemporary bagua consists of nine guas, each representing a critical aspect of life.

Pronounced *gwa*.

ideal home placement
The ideal location of a home on the building site; that is, the equivalent of being seated in a comfortable armchair with the Turtle (mountains) in the rear, the Phoenix (sun or river) in front, the Dragon and the Tiger (protective landforms) to the sides.

inauspicious
A term used in Feng Shui to denote unfavorable, undesirable, harmful influences and unsuccessful results.

integrative Feng Shui
An approach to Feng Shui that blends several schools, philosophies, and other methods.

lo-pan
The divination compass used for Compass School Feng Shui. Beginning as a magnetic needle floating in a bowl of water, the lo-pan evolved into a complex system of rings.

mantra
A word that is continually repeated, silently or out loud, to achieve a desired result.

maven
Someone who is an expert in a particular field.

Metal Element
One of the Five Elements. Metal is represented by the colors white, gold, and silver, as well as round shapes. Metal attributes are focus, strength, leadership, and inspiration.

mouth of chi
The main entrance door where chi, or energy, enters a structure. This is the front door as the architect or builder conceived of the home or building, even if it is not the primary entrance the occupants use when they enter.

poison arrow, *also called secret arrow, cutting chi, or poison arrow chi*
A sharp angle, point, edge, corner, or object that aims into a room or at a building and creates the negative energy called *sha chi*, which acts like an arrow aimed at a target. Poison arrows occur indoors when two walls or sharp edges of objects come together and point

out into a room, and outdoors where edges of a home or building point at another. Poison arrow chi represents harsh energy that can make a space uncomfortable or unhealthy.

power position
The most powerful location for a desk. This position is usually the area farthest from the door, and facing the door with your back to a solid wall. This position is considered the most powerful and safest since it provides a complete view of the room and the ability to see the door without being directly in line with it.

predecessor chi
The residual energy left behind by the previous occupants of a space.

red envelope tradition
Presentation of a red envelope containing some amount of money by a client to a Feng Shui practitioner as payment for services. This tradition was developed to respect and honor the information given. In Feng Shui For Real Life®, the practitioner gives information in a red envelope to the client to honor the relationship between them.

remedy
A Feng Shui change, cure, or adjustment.
  See also, *cure*.

Rule of 3Rs
A method of eliminating negative chi from a home or building that consists of: Replace, Repair, Remove. Three types of negative chi

that are removed when practicing this rule are: things you don't like, things that are broken, things that are cluttered.

sha chi
Negative energy. In situations where chi gets stuck or blocked, it becomes destructive, negative, harmful, and inauspicious *sha chi* energy. Sha chi can have extremely harsh effects on occupants.

shui
The Chinese word for water.
Pronounced *shway*.

space clearing
Any method used to get rid of negative, stagnant, or inauspicious energy in a space, whether current or residual from previous occupants. Methods include the use of sound, incense, smudging, ritual, or simply intention.

Tao, also *Taoism*
Means *the way* or *the path*. Taoism is the philosophical foundation work of most major religions in Asia. Modern Feng Shui defines Tao as continuity or connectedness with the natural world around us.
Pronounced *dow*.

Water Element
One of the Five Elements. Water energy is represented by the colors deep blue and black, and by wavy, patterned, or curvy shapes. The attributes of water are movement, flow, and communication.

wind chimes

A powerful Feng Shui remedy or cure to attract or *call* positive chi to a specific location.

Wood Element

One of the Five Elements. Wood energy is associated with the color green, and its shape is rectangular or columnar. The attributes of Wood are growth and expansion.

yang

The active, male side of the yin/yang balance. Yang qualities are light, activity, movement, rigidity, and strength. Yang needs to be balanced with opposite, or yin, qualities.

yin

The passive, female side of the yin/yang balance. Yin qualities are darkness, stillness, flexibility, and weakness. Yin needs to be balanced with opposite, or yang, qualities.

yin/yang balance

The balance of opposite characteristics in a space. In Feng Shui theory, all opposites are seen as complementary and inseparable forces that must be balanced.

GENERAL INDEX

F

Wright, Frank Lloyd, 11
Wright, Steven, 101
Wydra, Nancilee, 213

Y

yang, defined, 230
yin, defined, 230
Yin House Feng Shui, 23
yin/yang balance
    adjusting, 85–86
    in commercial spaces, 84–85
    defined, 230
    as power principle, 25
    theory described, 81–83, 83t7.1

CALENDAR INDEX

toilet seat lid, 159
"too much to do" feeling, 180
trash, 139, 163, 169
recycling bins, 199
trashcans, 169
traumatic experience, 181
travel, 150
trees, 162, 170
    bonsai as gifts, 203
    Christmas, 203
    pine, 163
    planted across from front door, 155
    stumps, 174
    taking down Christmas, 207
turquoise stone, 158
turtles, 156

U
underwear , 155
utility room, 180

V
vacation, 173, 175, 200
view, unattractive; correcting of, 170
vines, symbolism of, 174

W
wallets, 168, 204
watches, 204
water, 139, 147, 152, 157, 168, 171, 197
    draining of, 180
    leaking, 162, 192

Water Elements
    in the bathroom, 197
    to expand career success, 158
    and Hanukkah decorating, 205
    to help with writer's block, 182
wealth, 147, 159, 162, 163, 164, 175
    attracting of, 176
    cash flow, 181
    increasing of, 205
    and purse on floor, 162
wealth area, 157, 167, 182, 203
weight, losing, 164
whites, 157
wind chimes, 192, 194
windows, 155, 175
    dorm room, 186
    opening of, 191
    in relation to bed location, 193
Wood Elements
    to assist with writer's block, 182
    in the bathroom, 191
    in the dining room, 199
    to encourage happy and long marriage, 168
    to feel energized against cold, 142
    to help find a new job, 141
    to stimulate creativity and growth, 142
workspace, 141, 142, 150, 153, 157
writer's block, 182

ABOUT THE AUTHOR

Carol M. Olmstead, FSII, AKA The Feng Shui Maven, is a consultant, author, and lecturer specializing in practical, contemporary applications of Feng Shui for today's homes and offices. She conducts consultations and workshops for individuals, offices, businesses, and home buyers/sellers. Carol practices a contemporary version of Feng Shui that honors the essence of its 5,000-year-old Chinese heritage but focuses on the practical applications for our culture today. She uses her natural intuitive sense to bring easy-to-implement, real-world solutions to cure inauspicious situations and attract health, happiness, love, and prosperity.

Carol first learned about Feng Shui more than 12 years ago when she was a marketing communications consultant. She rearranged the furniture in her office and two weeks later signed a contract to consult for a week in Hawaii — which extended into a second week after she got there. Carol was convinced that Feng Shui made the difference! After extensive study with the Feng Shui Institute of America she became a Certified Feng Shui Practitioner, qualified to use the designation *FSII*. Carol was awarded Red Ribbon Professional status from the International Feng Shui Guild.

Carol and her Feng Shui For Real Life approach have been featured in *Cosmopolitan, The Washington Post, Washingtonian Magazine, The Chicago Tribune, The Georgetowner, Santa Fe New Mexican, Albuquerque Tribune, Philadelphia Inquirer, Bethesda Magazine, The Hill* newspaper, *Crystal City Magazine, Baltimore Magazine, Prevention Books, Telecommuting for Dummies*, and online home decorating and remodeling websites. She is a frequent guest on TV and broadcast and Internet radio. In addition to providing home and office consultations, Carol has presented workshops and classes to diverse corporate, nonprofit, and academic groups across the country.

CAN'T GET ENOUGH FENG SHUI?

Check out *www.FengShuiForRealLife.com*, your source for accurate information about the modern applications of this ancient practice.

This website includes:
- •Feng Shui Basics
- •Articles About Feng Shui
- •Success Stories
- •Regional Aspects of Feng Shui
- •Workshops and Seminars
- •Online Store

Want more **free** Feng Shui tips? Subscribe to the monthly *Feng Shui For Real Life E-zine*. Go to *www.FengShuiForRealLife.com* and click on the blue "subscribe" box in the lower left hand corner of the home page.

WHAT THEY ARE SAYING

Carol M. Olmstead has taught thousands of people the simple secrets of using Feng Shui to attract wealth, harmony, and love into their lives. Carol is Certified by the Feng Shui Institute of America and earned Red Ribbon Professional status from the International Feng Shui Guild.

Here is what people are saying about Carol's real-life method of using the practical magic of Feng Shui:

As a psychologist I transform lives using the powers of intention and attraction. Working with Carol took me to the next level, bringing my outer life into alignment with what I am creating inside. Her practical application of Feng Shui is essential to the transformation process!
  ~ Dr. Mark, Transformational Coach

Living with Feng Shui really helps me feel like I have more influence over the events of my life. Just getting the changes started has made things feel better, and the kids are already happier. My thanks to Carol for that.
  ~ Joan G., Restaurant Owner

I put my house on the market last weekend, held an Open House on Sunday, received two offers on Tuesday, and sold it on Wednesday for what I wanted—even though the market is slow! Settlement is coinciding with the move to my new home and I am happy and relieved. I thank Carol for all of her help and recommendations to make my house sell so quickly!
  ~ Marian L., Realtor

I can say with absolute certainty that my business is thriving and growing since I first met Carol. The Feng Shui process was fun and her continued input as changes have occurred in the business has been extremely helpful. My employees feel that the space is now more conducive to their productivity and has enhanced their daily work experience.

~ Barry R., Furniture Designer

Carol's recommendations made a lot of sense, so I implemented them. And wouldn't you know within two weeks I met THE guy. Carol's advice to throw out all those letters from my last relationship made more room, and the little fun adjustments in my bedroom probably didn't hurt, either.

~ Jennifer L., Teacher

We marked the missing areas of our home as you suggested and already it feels more comfortable and replenishing. I realized how the busy-ness of life has kept us from moving forward and it was showing in how we were keeping the house. And it certainly helped my husband to hear someone else tell him to clear out his clutter, both emotional and actual. Thanks, Carol, for the jumpstart.

~ Melissa W., Bank Vice President

31

Give your home a thorough cleaning
so you can begin the new year
with a clean slate.

Coming Soon!
THE FENG SHUI FOR REAL LIFE TIP-A-DAY CALENDAR

from

Carol M. Olmstead, Certified Feng Shui Practitioner

Use the power of Feng Shui to make simple, practical changes in your life one day at a time. The **Feng Shui For Real Life Tip-A-Day Calendar** gives you easy-to-follow and low-cost tips for every day of the year, including leap year.

Adapted from the **Feng Shui Quick Guide for Home and Office**, this calendar features a year of advice for attracting wealth, revving up your love life, creating family harmony, finding a better job. The tips cover all of the seasons and all of the adventures and misadventures of your life. Liberally sprinkled through the calendar are success stories from real people who used these tips to improve their lives.

Here are a few sample tips:

January 1: *Move 27 things to encourage something new to happen in the coming year.*

April 15: *If you paid too much in taxes this year, place three valuable coins in the wealth area of your house to help activate the flow of prosperity.*

December 31: *Decorate your home for New Year's Eve with gold and silver, the colors of valuable coins, symbolizing your intention to attract wealth in the coming year.*

Pre-order the **Feng Shui For Real Life Tip-A-Day Calendar** now for a 10% discount.

To order, visit *http://www.FengShuiForRealLife.com/calendar*